En Route to Eternity

Further Along the Road

En Route to Eternity

Further Along the Road

The Story of My Life

by Ronda De Sola Chervin

The Miriam Press
Saint Louis, Missouri

The Miriam Press
4120 West Pine Blvd.
St. Louis, MO 63108
www.hebrewcatholic.net

ISBN: 978-0939409-12-9
Library of Congress Control Number: 2022940732

Contents

Introduction 1

A Note about the Hebrew Catholic Perspective. 5

Newly Widowed. 11

A Consecrated Life 17

Seeking Community 23

Teaching and Writing 27

Journal Excerpts (1998 - 2002) 37

"God Alone Is Enough" 85

Last Teaching Position 145

Retired Great-Grandmother 151

Appendix I: Prayer for Widows 159

Appendix II: Stations of the Cross for Widows 161

Appendix III: Pop Psychology and Catholic Spirituality 169

Appendix IV: Books by Ronda Chervin. 177

Introduction

"The truth shall set you free!" (John 8:32)

A t almost 82 years old, writing about my life is different than at 56 when I wrote *En Route to Eternity*.

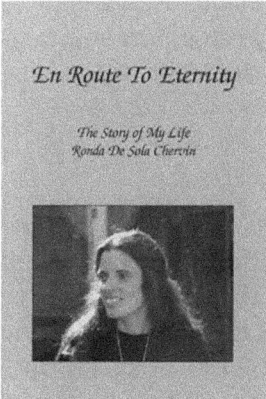

Here are 2 reasons - one obvious, and one more interesting:

I can hardly remember what day of the week it is, no less the exact sequence of events in 1995 and following!

Instead of life being like walking on a calendar, one event after another, thinking about the past is more like viewing images in a kaleidoscope, flittering and merging.

My present spiritual director challenged me to see if there was a theme for these last 25 years. What has God been trying to teach me?

After praying about it, I came up with 3 themes:

- "The drama queen heroine, Ronda, always gets check-mated by life!"
- "Every utopia becomes a gulag!"
- "God alone is enough!"

In case the words describing these truths are not self-evident, here is my opening explanation of them.

Drama Queen Scenarios:

If my conscious or unconscious view of life is that I am the heroine of the drama of my life, and everyone else is a secondary character or only a bit player, saying and doing what will enhance my role, then I will be angry, anxious, and depressed every day of my life! Why? Because the others want to be themselves the hero or heroine with me as the secondary character or bit player.

On the other hand, when God graces me into thinking that He is the

1

center of life, and we, his followers, need to become secondary characters holding hands, trying to speak and act as He wishes the drama to proceed, life can be much less frustrating.

Utopias and Gulags:

The formula that every utopia becomes a gulag was coined by Gary McCabe, one of my mentors when I taught at Holy Apostles College and Seminary in Connecticut (2009-2017). It means that trying to create perfect political States or even perfect lay religious communities leads not to bliss but to lives victimized by the leaders, as in the Soviet gulags (prison camps).

God Alone is Enough:

This famous dictum attributed to St. Teresa of Avila means that we can only become holy if detached from everything in the created world. As Jesus taught: "in the world, but not of the world." When we are overly attached to anything in the world, all the way from candy to wanting spectacular visible graces, we can never be at peace. Only the acceptance of unavoidable crosses and the hope of heaven give us true joy on our earthly journey.

So, a woman of 81 is rarely the heroine of any drama. But I certainly tried to be after becoming a widow in 1993! And you will probably find my accounts of these failures to be amusing. Consider that twelve men I thought might be wonderful second husbands rejected me!

The utopias I tried to be part of, or found, were Catholic communities. Out of love for those involved, I will not name them or describe the "gulag" aspects of these failed attempts. Nonetheless, you will probably find what I write to be helpful in either finding or constructing better ones, or resigning yourself more willingly to relative loneliness!

When I tell you about how Jesus has tried to lead me in the direction of embracing God alone as enough, I hope you will be as inspired as I have been, en route to eternity, destined for the bliss of divine love for an infinite amount of time in heaven.

My plan is that *Further Along the Road* will not be a year-by-year diary-type book about events. Due to some family criticism of my autobiography *En Route to Eternity* up to 1994, about inclusion of matters some did not want to see in print, I will not include those ongoing dramas. This decision saddens me because it means that I cannot express here my ardent love of my twin, my daughters, each grand-child, and now great-grandchildren!

I could write a lot about the marvelous virtues of my family members, but I find, sometimes, that when speaking of them positively, some can dislike my particular take on these same virtues. So, instead of including their stories with mine, *Further Along the Road* will be more of a chroni-cle of my own personal struggles of those years of my life from 57-82, and how I thought Jesus got me through.

My Twin Daughters, Carla and Diana, 2014

Still, so you won't think of me as a dedicated widow with no family, I am appending right at the start, here, some favorite photos of them.

Another caveat. I have had many wonderful friends in my life. The names of some of these are in this Story of my later years because those persons are related on some event or insight I am describing. If you are one of my friends whose name isn't in this book, it is not be-cause you are not dear to me, but simply that our bond was not specifi-cally related to some point I was making!

Jesus once seemed to "tell" me in interior prayer: "Ronda, you know how you love to create classes, TV programs, radio shows, parish workshops? I would love to create you as a real saint. Won't you let me?"

"It's not possible! I'm too awful." I replied.

"Try!" He seemed to insist.

Here we go!

Diana's family, 2010

Carla's family, 2017

Martina, youngest grand-child of Carla and Steve

3

Some of Ronda Chervin's Early Works: 1978–1993

Ronda Chervin, Mary Neill & You
The Woman's Tale
A Journal of Inner Exploration

Bringing the Mother with You

Hungry for Heaven

The Story of Charles Rich, Contemplative

Am I a Charismatic

Feminine, Free, & Faithful

Ronda Chervin

Victory Over Death

Ronda Chervin

the ingrafting
the conversion stories of ten hebrew-catholics
edited by ronda chervin

GREAT SAINTS GREAT FRIENDS

Prayers of the **Women Mystics**
Ronda De Sola Chervin

Treasury of **Women Saints**
The Stories of Over 200 Women, Including Mothers, Prophets, and Interior Women of the Spirit
Ronda De Sola Chervin

Quotable Saints
Ronda De Sola Chervin

Spiritual Friendship

Woman to Woman

LOVE OF WISDOM
An Introduction to CHRISTIAN PHILOSOPHY
Ronda Chervin, Ph.D.
Eugene Kevane, Ph.D.
Ignatius

RONDA CHERVIN

See Appendix IV on page 177 for a full list with dates

A Note about the Hebrew Catholic Perspective

"Shout for joy, O Daughter Zion." (Zephaniah 3:14)

Since this sequel will be a publication of The Miriam Press of the Association of Hebrew Catholics, I want to write a little about my cultural Jewishness as it has influenced my life.

Most Jews who become Catholics were brought up with at least a minimum of Jewish religious practice. And this even if their parents were on the verge of being agnostic. If only Chanukah and Passover, and, maybe, Rosh Hashana. But in my case, there was absolutely not a bit of Jewish religious practice, as all but one Christian grand-mother were militant atheists.

Nonetheless, what is now called cultural Judaism has permeated my life-story. There may be some of you readers who call yourselves Hebrew Catholics, who will identify with parts of this aspect of my life. On the other hand, some of you may feel very differently. I find there are many Jews and some Hebrew Catholics who do not at all fit the stereotype that describes me so well.

I am assuming that the only readers of *Further Along the Road* will be those who read my autobiography up to the year 1994. If not, please read it first.

However, just in case you read it decades ago and have forgotten a lot of it, here is a brief summary of my life up until my husband's death in 1993.

I was baptized a Catholic at age 21. Most of my family were atheists of several generations back, but of Jewish cultural background. In 1959, I converted through miracles and also intellectual arguments by the great defenders of the faith. Recently I wrote a book with co-author Sebastian Mahfood entitled *Why be an Atheist if???* I have an interesting chapter about the conversions of other atheists you might find fascinating, and Dr. Mahfood, with more of a science background, deals incisively with arguments against God coming out of false ideas about science. You might want to try it out on atheist acquaintances.

My godmother, Leni Schwarz, was from a similar background. She was the child of a German doctor who was atheistic but of Jewish ancestry. She, like me, became a Catholic in her 20's. This was when marrying Professor Balduin Schwarz, my future godfather. They immigrated to the United States during World War II. I met them at Fordham University when I studied there.

Godparents, Leni and Balduin Schwarz

After my conversion, I was looking for a saintly Catholic husband. It would take me years to realize that it was hard for devout Catholic young men to understand a woman like me. Even though my wish was to become a good Christian wife and mother, my character was marred by factors almost impossible for any of them to understand.

For instance, how can anybody brought up Christian, or of strong Jewish belief for that matter, imagine a childhood where the ideal was Nietzsche's superman vs. Jesus or Isaiah?

We were taught that the greatest value in life was to be smart or creative or both. Goodness, self-sacrifice, humble obedience to authority? Those were the traits of conventional, stupid, weak individuals who didn't have smarts or artistic genius.

As a result, even when that perspective had been overturned by love of Jesus and the saints, I found self-sacrifice, especially in little physical things such as mopping a floor, almost unbearable!

So, God check-mated my desire for a saintly Catholic husband by sending me an atheist with an orthodox Jewish background, who was a divorced playboy salesman!

I was attracted to my brilliant, creative, interesting Jewish atheist husband because he had those traits I was brought up to love. I also wanted the Jewish warmth he possessed. Years later, I would describe him as a mix of the character Tevye, of *Fiddler on the Roof*, and John Milton, the English poet.

Martin Chervin was given a dispensation from his first non-religious marriage to marry me in the Church in 1962, and he became a Catholic himself when he was in his 60's. You can read about his remarkable conversion in the book *Bread from Heaven, Stories of Jews who found the Messiah.* He wrote a book entitled *Children of the Breath.* It is a fictional account of all that might have been talked about during the 40 Days of the Temptation of Jesus in the desert. A basic theme is Satan insisting that Jesus could not successfully proclaim that people who needed to be wolves to survive should, instead, become lambs. In the final scene, we see Jesus setting forth to prove that being a lamb is better.

In 1963, we had twin girls, Carla and Diana, many miscarriages, and then Charles, our son, 8 years later. My own twin, Carla De Sola, became a Catholic a few years after I did. She became a world-famous sacred dancer. My mother later became a Catholic, also.

For many decades, I enjoyed the mentorship of Charles Rich, a lay contemplative Hebrew Catholic who came out of a village in Hungary much like that in *Fiddler on the Roof.* I edited several of his books and compiled letters he wrote to me over the years. Check him out on my website www.rondachervin.com under Friends of Charles Rich.

Another wonderful Hebrew Catholic friendship was with the Schneir family – parents: Cathy and Harvey, nurse and doctor and pro-life activists, and their children who all became strong Catholic witnesses to the goodness of family life. Greetings to you, Matthew Schneir, my godson, if you read this someday.

The growth of the Association of Hebrew Catholics, a ministry to Jews who are looking for Jesus and for a Church and a support group for Catholics of Jewish ancestry, was a wonderful new group on the Catholic scene. Of course, those of you reading this book know about this ministry because it is published by The Miriam Press.

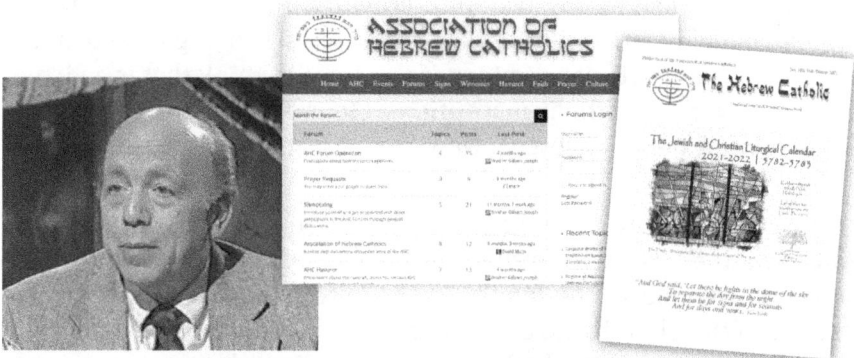

David Moss and the Association of Hebrew Catholics forum and newsletter.

I became the godmother of Rosalind Moss (the sister of David Moss, who is the President of the Association of Hebrew Catholics). Rosalind was first a Reform Jew, then a "Jews for Jesus" convert, then an Evangelical minister, then finally a Roman Catholic, an apologist for Catholic Answers, an EWTN presenter, and is now the founder of a community of Sisters. (See https://motherofisraelshope.org/)

I am also the godmother of a Jewish college student of mine, Russell. Another godchild is Tzvi Schnee, a Messianic Jewish scholar living in Arizona. I am a confirmation sponsor of Gail Demarest, a traditional Latin-Mass Catholic, living in Arkansas.

I met Gail while living in a small town where there were two famous Hebrew Catholics: Marty Barrack (https://secondexodus.com/) and Ariela LeGendre.

When visiting a daughter living in New Hampshire, I greatly enjoyed the friendship of Roy Schoeman, then living in Boston; Roy is a Jewish convert who has written important books such as *Salvation is from the Jews.* (See https://www.salvationisfromthejews.com/)

At Holy Apostles, I was happy for the friendship of Dr. Cynthia Toolin, a theologian and convert coming from a Jewish background.

As the years go by, a factor in my life that I have become much more aware of is how much my Jewish cultural background impacts my life in the Church.

Somewhat humorously I like to say, I have all the most hated traits of New York Jews, even though I am a Catholic.

"What?"

Well, yes. I am loud, pushy, and scheming. I explain it partly by my youth spent pushing my way into crowded New York City subway trains. On the positive side, as with many Jews, I am highly articulate, relational, and...self-deprecatory, if you want to think that is a virtue! Trying to work in Catholic institutions, I found it hard to fit in. I didn't know why. A new-age Jewish New York psycho-therapist diagnosed it this way:

"In Jewish culture, coming out of the ghettos in Europe, everyone talked all the time, within their enclave, about what was happening in the towns and in the family. In the predominantly Irish Catholic culture of the Church, the background is of putting on a genial façade and plotting behind the hedges against the English over-lords. Since you don't get to know what your Catholic administrators think, you are always anxious."

Once, as a widow, while trying out a new possible community setting, Jesus seemed to tell me, "Don't try to fit in. Shine forth!"

Besides all this, I am not even like the most famous Hebrew Catholic saints. For example, so articulate St. Paul champions gentleness and meekness, not the aggressive, pushy, self-assertiveness that I exhibit all too often. St. Edith Stein, the woman atheist philosopher convert, who I believe interceded for my conversion years ago, was known for her diplomatic contemplative personality. Blurt out whatever I think is true, is more my way. Unless gifted with graces of infused prayer, my attention span when in a chapel is about 3 minutes. Blessed Francis Libermann, the Jewish convert founder of the Holy Ghost missionary order, counseled others even though he, himself, was afflicted with epilepsy and nervous anxiety. I am usually much too busy trying to bombard others with my truths to understand their individual problems.

All right, already! I wouldn't have so many loving family members, godchildren, friends, disciples, and fans if I had no good traits!

Pray for me!

Come to think of it, I do identify with two big, big, Jewish ancestry saints: Teresa of Avila and John of the Cross. In those times, people who were practicing Catholics but had Jewish grandparents, for instance, who had converted in the past, didn't advertise this fact. But research has shown that Teresa and John were of converso backgrounds. Now, what I identify with in Teresa is her chatty writing style. And with both of them, it is their tremendous yearning for closeness to God.

Once, I was praying during adoration at a chapel of contemplative nuns of the order founded by Conchita of Mexico. The nuns in the chapel were totally silent and still.

I thought:

"Jesus, I can never be holy. I am such a jumpy dingbat!"

Jesus seemed to tell me: "I didn't create you to be a contemplative of this kind. Your restlessness is part of the yearning of the Jewish people."

It happens that my best friend, another widow dedicated to the

Lord, Marti Armstrong, grew up in a neighborhood where she was friendly with lots of Jewish families. She thinks that when we Jews become Catholic, we bring wonderful traits into the Church such as passionate zeal, honesty about our own failings, and a typical Jewish form of humor and warmth.

I do well in prayer picturing Jesus, Mary, and Joseph as overflowing with that Jewish type of zeal and warmth.

Newly Widowed

"Take care of widows and orphans." (James 1:27)

The first volume of my autobiography, *En Route to Eternity*, ends with the tragic death by suicide of our son, Charlie, and then with Martin's death in 1993. Here is a photo of Charlie just before he died.

My son, Charlie.

At that time, my husband and I were living with our adult daughter Carla, her husband, Peter and her first two children: Nicholas and Alexander. We resided in Woodland Hills, California. I was teaching at St. John's Seminary of the Archdiocese of Los Angeles.

What was my life like at that time?

My health was not so good. I had surgery to remove one breast that was cancerous in 1989. I didn't realize I also had the beginnings of late onset diabetes (called Type 2). I was teaching at St. John's Seminary in Camarillo, California. This was my second big job after seventeen years of teaching at Loyola Marymount University in Los Angeles. Teaching seminarians was especially suited to my gifts because, even though I taught the standard courses in philosophy at the University, my method was to blend together insights from philosophy, psychology, and spirituality.

Now, the late-vocation men at St. John's seminary had to take some 10 courses in philosophy, and most of them were not especially philosophical, but were very pastorally-oriented. So, for example, my illustrating philosophical truths with examples from the daily life of typical parishioners was helpful to them. In a course such as philosophy of the human person, I would summarize differences between Plato and Aristotle, but would also teach about the concepts as illustrated by conflicts between spouses in a marriage. The period of teaching at the seminary was also a time when some of my most popular books were being published by Servant Press. Two titles you might be familiar with are *Treasury of Women Saints,* and *Catholic Customs and Traditions* (written with one of my daughters, Carla Conley).

The book most of my readers think is my best came out of struggling with the death of my son. Experiencing such acute anguish over that event, I decided to research the saints to see how they got through the worst sufferings. The book that resulted is called *The Kiss from the Cross: A Saint for Every Kind of Suffering* (Ann Arbor, Michigan: Servant Publications), 1994. It was reprinted in 2015 under the title *Avoiding Bitterness in Suffering: How Our Heroes in Faith Found Peace amid Sorrow,* by Sophia Institute Press (Manchester, New Hampshire), 2015.

The biggest change in our lives after the deaths of Charlie and Martin was the Northridge earthquake in 1994. Only 2 months after my husband's death came this huge quake. We lived only 20 minutes from the epi-center. Terrified by the quake itself and then the aftershocks which continued for months, my daughter Carla, and her husband, decided to move away. They got in the van and went East looking for good places to live. When they hit Sedona, Arizona, they thought it was the most beautiful of places they had ever seen. Peter quit his job as an aerospace computer engineer at Hughes aircraft and started writing a book about his expertise. Carla did contract computer work while raising the children.

What about me? We had moved to California from New York in the '70's because of Martin's asthma, hoping warmer weather would help. But I had always wished I could have taught at Franciscan University of Steubenville in Ohio.

Now that I couldn't live near the Seminary with my family, since they were leaving for Arizona, what could be better than a place like Franciscan University? Magisterial, charismatic, and also Franciscan! It also happened that the Chair of the Philosophy Department was Dr. Michael Healey, a former student of mine.

More about that job and living situation in the next chapter.

Now, what about those themes of mine: Drama Queen, Utopian, and God Alone is Enough? I have long believed that God permitted me to be an extreme of many things so that as a teacher, speaker, and media presenter, I could help others understand their own less dramatic experiences.

Many widows look for second husbands, but few are rejected *twelve* times!

You need a bit of background to understand. As chronicled in *En Route to Eternity*, my marriage was less than ideal. A spiritual director once chided me for thinking of it as a failure.

"Did you help him reach heaven?"

"Yes."

"Then it wasn't a failure!"

We did experience an unexpected and wonderful, total, unconditional forgiveness in the last decade of our marriage. (see *En Route to Eternity*, p. 112.) Just the same, because Martin often had possibly death-dealing asthma attacks, he thought he would die every night. He used to ask me what I would do after he died.

"I'll become a nun."

"You can't become a nun!"

"Why not?"

"Because you ARE a nun," he joked.

He did not mean this in a positive way.

Actually, I wasn't planning to become a nun. In the back of my mind, I had a short list of single devout Catholic men who I imagined might want to be my second husband.

Here is where the "drama queen" scenarios come in.

Now, you will be disappointed. No names! These poor guys suffered enough dealing with my false hopes and complicated personality without having to read, even from eternity if they have passed on, my descriptions of their foibles. But, I think, #1, who has long gone to his eternal reward, will not mind this one anecdote. When he heard I was flying from Los Angeles to visit him, he checked himself into the hospital so I wouldn't be able to find him!

Here is the drama queen pattern, with overtones of utopianism, that I detect in hindsight.

From the years when I was married. I have good memories of wonderful encounters with single, older Catholic men.

I try not to think of any of the defects of these same possible second husbands. Utopian?

We arrange a meeting during which I bubble over effusively about each one's marvelous traits and scheme about "utopian?" ways we might live once married, in the Church, of course. Each one finds polite ways to escape while still remaining friends. It was only years later that it occurred to me that a man who has never married in 70 years, it's not because he didn't meet me! Or, that single men who gravitate toward married women to enjoy the warmth, may "run like hell" if we are free!

Now I am laughing, but at the time it was very painful, especially when my favorites rejected me. I had a longer relationship with a widower, but that didn't work for other reasons. Throughout the years after becoming a widow, I have other takes on all this. In the words of one of my daughters: "We always thought Dad was the only man in the world who could have been married to you." I mean, heh, how many men, even if devoutly Catholic, want to live with the residual characteristics of a New York Jewish philosopher? The bad Jewish traits, such as incessant talking, pushy attempts to micromanage them...combined with the philosophical traits such as preferring analyzing everything in life to enjoying life, or writing articles while the hamburgers burn in the frying pan?

Or, on the spiritual side, could Jesus, who would become my second bridegroom a few years after these rejections, have permitted me to try to grab men the least likely to marry me so I would, by default, choose Him?

A good fruit of my struggles as a new widow came from researching the widow saints to see how they got through that time in their lives.

A Widow's Walk: Encouragement, Comfort, and Wisdom from the Widow-Saints (Huntington, Indiana: Our Sunday Visitor) was published in 1998. (With the help of Heidi Hess Saxton, this was reprinted in a revised edition related more to the grieving process for widows by Simon Peter Press [Johnette Benkovic's publishing house] under the title *Walk With Me, Jesus: A Widow's Journey*, in 2008.)

Until I began reading up on them, I had no idea how many widow saints there were, and how diverse were their choices. I traced their griefs - most grieved, though some felt liberated who had very bad spouses. I found fascinating how some became founders of religious orders, others became contemplative mystics, and one reached out to Communists in the Spanish Civil War.

14

I also wrote a prayer for widows and a Stations of the Cross for widows. (See the Appendix of this book.)

What about the "God Alone is Enough" theme as it concerns the time of my early widowhood? It happens that shortly after becoming a widow, I assembled a book of my journals entitled *Becoming a Handmaid of the Lord* (1977-1996). The excerpts I have placed later here manifest the way I thought Jesus was "speaking to me" during the first year of this tumultuous time of my life. Now, I realize that some readers are "allergic" to anyone claiming that God talks to him or her. I always include in books of such "messages" that in my case, these are almost never audible words but are rather thoughts in my heart. I never claim they have to have been directly from Jesus. I believe they are, because they are more beautiful than anything I have ever written. Such words in the heart are by no means proof of holiness – first of all, because they can come from Satan masquerading as an angel of light; and secondly, because some doctors of the Church think they are designed to help weak beginners and that dark nights of the soul are even greater proofs of God's favor!

So, when I cite such words in my heart from Jesus, I do so because they helped me, and if truly from Him, may help you, also.

Ronda: "Here I am, Jesus, your weak, silly, widow. With Martin gone, I feel like a balloon floating on the ceiling or like a rowboat with one oar only, so my paddling just makes the boat go in circles instead of ahead."

Jesus: "Even though you're so weak, I can still use you to reach others as a Catholic teacher. When you feel panic, run into My arms like a panting dog might do. As I calm you, I fill you with My soothing love."

When I think about the single life, Jesus seems to ask, "Wouldn't I be enough?"

Mary seems to tell me that even though she lost the earthly presence of Joseph and of her son, Jesus, that God gave her John and the other apostles, and He is clearly, also, giving me other sons.

An insight from one such son friend: "It is not so much that we glorify the dead when we lose a spouse, but that when we are no longer the victim of their faults, it is easier for us to perceive how much their strengths outweighed their flaws." I later came to enunciate that insight with these words of admonition to married couples: "After you become a widow, you realize that the absence of annoyance is not joy."

Before becoming a widow, I imagined that it would be terrific grief, and then I would get on with my life. Now, after 25 years of widowhood, I realize it is very different for most widows. There are sporadic waves of grief. Then there are unexpected memories where joys of the past become so real, we could taste them. I know two widows who experienced the spiritual presence of their husbands the moment they died and then constantly around them for the rest of their lives! Someone who knew my husband well can sometimes tell me something I didn't know that gives me new insight and forgiveness for things I didn't understand at the time.

In my case, Jesus seemed to suggest that I should stop making endless phone calls to be sure I have others to grab in my shakiness. "When you are frightened, crawl up on My lap. Watch and see each day how I show you My love through others."

In the midst of all my planning, I imagine my son and husband looking down at me and cheering me on. Instead of thinking of myself as single, maybe think of myself as a pilgrim?

A Consecrated Life

"I exalt with joy in Yahweh...like a bride adorned in her jewels."
(Isaiah 61:10)
"You are a pearl of great price." (Matthew 13:45-46)

In the fall of 1994, I started teaching at Franciscan University of Steubenville in Ohio. In the next chapter about seeking community, I will write about the truly utopian features of this amazing Catholic place. In this chapter, I want instead to trace the beginnings of my vocation as a consecrated woman, going way back through my growth in spirituality over my many years as a married wife and mother.

What is spirituality? One of the best definitions I heard was "the way to God." In my life, we are not talking about what some today call spirituality in contrast to religion, as in the popular proclamation: "I am into spirituality, not religion." Such a stance included a misunderstanding of the word "religion" which is derived from "religio," meaning a connection. If religion is a connection to the true God, then it is not an opposite to spirituality. Rather, spirituality is a part of religion. In the Catholic religion, spirituality can be viewed as the result of the gifts of the Holy Spirit. In ordinary usage in our Church, it means a particular way of pursuing holiness, as in Marian spirituality, Benedictine spirituality, Franciscan spirituality, Dominican spirituality, Ignatian spirituality...and many more.

Now, I was brought into the Church in the Von Hildebrand circle, most of whom, like Dietrich Von Hildebrand, were lay oblates of Benedictine monasteries in different parts of the world. Benedictine spirituality for lay people is outwardly expressed in honoring first the Holy Liturgy of the Mass and then praying, daily as much as possible, the 7 sets of psalms, readings, and petitions of the Liturgy of the Hours. Though not yet an oblate of a monastery, in my first years of being a Catholic in the 1960's, I followed these daily practices. Since these liturgies were in Latin, which I had never studied, I read them out of books with the English on the companion page of each volume. As a philosophy student, the aspect of the faith that I loved most was TRUTH. Jesus was the incarnate truth that was God the Father. I remember being startled when my godfather, Balduin Schwarz, a philosophy professor, asked me whether during the day I had a time of praying silently in my own words. It hadn't occurred to me, and I found that when I tried, it was difficult. Why mutter things in my own paltry lingo when there were perfect words in the liturgical books? When I finally found God as personal love, I characterized the change in my spirituality in this way: "Up until now, praying was for me like standing on tippy-toes trying to reach God in the sky. Now I find Him right in my heart."

What brought about the change? It came for me in 1969, with the graces of the charismatic gifts of the Holy Spirit. If interested, you can read the whole story in a book I wrote that was published in 1978: *Why I am a Catholic Charismatic.* That life-changing experience is also described in *En Route to Eternity.* By no means did this breakthrough alienate me from daily Holy Mass or the Liturgy of the Hours. In fact, shortly afterward, I became an Oblate of the Monastery of St. Andrew's in Valyermo, California. The liturgical prayers simply became more personal.

For years, I went once a week to the charismatic prayer meetings at Loyola Marymount University of Los Angeles where I was teaching. Even though my favorite music will always be classical, especially Bach, Mozart, and Beethoven, I did also learn to love the praise-filled charismatic hymns they played at prayer meetings. For me, in some way, swaying to those rhythms with upraised arms seemed like a throw-back to some part of my unknown Jewish Chasidic ancestry. Zephaniah 3 includes the words: "Shout for joy, O Daughter Zion." A popular charismatic song based on these words is "And the Father will Dance." Even though "Zion" stands for not only the Jewish people but also the Christian people, I like to relate daughter Zion to myself as a female Jewish lover of Jesus. Whenever possible at charismatic conferences when I finish my talk, I urge the music ministers to play "And the Father will Dance" and then cajole as many as possible in the audience to get up and do an Israeli-type round dance to the music.

Another welcome change came with the practice of laying hands on others. Rejected by some Catholics as "touchy-feely," I found it expansive. It took me out of my intellectual, highly analytic and philosophical personality into a spiritual motherhood where touch was part of a compassionate embrace of other Catholics.

Is there more to Catholic spirituality than all this?

Yes, there is, as I found out in the year 1980. A few women in my parish who were part of the Blue Army of Our Lady of Fatima asked me if I wanted to host the pilgrim Statue of Mary in my home. When making a consecration to the heart of Mary, I was suddenly invaded by contemplative visions and locutions. You may read more about the amazing graces that followed in *En Route to Eternity* (p. 112 and following). Years later, when working for an M.A. in spirituality at the Notre Dame Apostolic Institute in Arlington, Virginia, I would learn that what came to me in those graces was part of what the Church calls *bridal mysticism*.

Now, the word "bridal" might lead you to think that bridal mysticism is only for vowed religious Sisters. Not so! Probably the greatest spiritual writer on bridal mysticism is St. John of the Cross! Bridal mysticism is characterized by an ecstatic sense of Jesus wanting to flood the soul with supernatural love. Why? Partly to express His love, but also so that we may overflow with that divine love to all we meet. It culminates in what is called the spiritual marriage of the soul with Jesus. Now, being graced with bridal mysticism does not mean that because of such a heavenly embrace there are none of the struggles and pain of our usual life on earth. On the contrary, the closer we are drawn to Jesus, the more we are also drawn into His sufferings. Pain and Joy seem to be opposites, but they are not incompatible. Just think about your ordinary daily life. Can't you be delighted by a beautiful sunrise even if you also have a headache?

So, did I reach such a peak as spiritual marriage? I think so, but it was in an unexpected way.

After all the rejections by men I went through as a widow when I was teaching at Franciscan University of Steubenville, I met a woman, Yvonne Rosedale, who was in the process of founding a religious community for older women called Handmaids of Nazareth. Yvonne was the mother of a student at Franciscan whom she was visiting. She heard about my many books and asked me if I would help her write the rule for this emerging community. This was in the year 1995. I said I would be happy to do so. One morning shortly afterwards, I came early to Mass. Here is how I described in my journal what happened, to be found on p. 260-261 in my book *Becoming a Handmaid of the Lord*: "Jesus put me in a deep, breathy quiet. An interior vision is one where the recipient sees in his or her heart, as it were, some supernatural being. I saw Jesus – the face was that of El Greco's Christ imprinted on Veronica's Veil. (In a few pages you can see a photo of this portrait of Jesus by El Greco.) I am in a lacy wedding gown. He is wearing a bridegroom tuxedo. I sense Him seizing my heart to be His bride. I also have a sense of the pain of invisible stigmata in my hands and feet. He kisses my forehead and offers me a ring made of hair." I asked Him if He wanted me to be a handmaid in the community Yvonne Rosedale was founding. He seemed to say "Yes, so you could be totally focused on Me."

Later, I thought that the interior vision of Him in a tuxedo was a bit droll! I asked Him why He chose that way to appear to me. He seemed to say: "When I tried to espouse you without that conventional image, you were not sure it was a marriage, so this is a little joke to convince you." Then I felt deep, deep, peace and joy and Mary's mantle over me.

Later in this period of my life, I had this thought about locutions and humor: Several times I have received rather humorous replies to questions of mine, seemingly from members of the Trinity. Since as a Christian philosopher, I am focused on the august sublimity of the divine, I usually doubt such words in the heart are really from them. However, recently I have been reading the locutions and visions of a canonized mystic. These include quite a surprising number of humorous ones. Even if God is sublime, surely I am not, so why shouldn't God lighten me up a little from time to time? The topic of humor in things I believe have been messages from on high, might it fall under the Thomistic truth that "everything is received according to the nature of the recipient"? Since I am a funny person who giggles often and causes others to laugh a lot as well, maybe that is why the truths God wants to reach me with sometimes come out with a humorous twist.

In the next chapter on seeking community, I will say more about trying to become a Handmaid of Nazareth. It didn't work out. However, while still in formation in Yvonne's order with the name of Ronda Marie of the Precious Blood, I did make a private promise to belong to Jesus as my second bridegroom.

What is a private promise? Without being part of a religious community, anyone who is not married can make a promise, approved by a priest, committing to not re-marrying and living a chaste life in union with Jesus. Here is a photo of what I wrote down as my promise. It constitutes a consecration:

August 23, 1996

My Beautiful Jesus,
I come before you,
a daughter of Zion, a widow,
redeemed in Your precious blood,
to consecrate my heart to you,
under the guidance of the Holy Spirit,
and obedient to Him,
For The rest of my life

in a private vow of ~~celibacy~~ chastity
as your bride.
in a vow of simplicity
For The sake of the poor
I wish to live as your handmaid
in The image of your Blessed Mother.
I beg you to heal & purify my heart
that There may be nothing inside
but love for god & each person
I encounter.   Amen

Sister Ronda Marie
of The Precious Blood

My consecration letter.

21

Some Works from the Next Decade: 1994-2004

Bread From Heaven
stories of Jews who found the Messiah

IDEAS FOR FAMILIES

The Book of
Catholic Customs and Traditions

Enhancing Holidays,
Special Occasions,
& Family Celebrations

Ronda De Sola Chervin
and Carla Conley

A MOTHER'S TREASURY of PRAYERS

RONDA DE SOLA

The Fabric

of Our Lives

Assembled and Edited by

Ronda Chervin

The Kiss from the Cross

Saints for Every Kind of Suffering

Ronda De Sola Chervin

Becoming a Handmaid of the Lord

From the Journals of
Ronda De Sola Chervin
1977–1995

VOYAGE to INSIGHT

BY RONDA CHERVIN, PH.D.
AND LOIS AUGUST JANIS

Freed to Love

HOLDING HANDS WITH GOD

Seeking Christ in the Crosses & Joys of Aging

By
Ronda Chervin
CMJ Marian Publishers

Taming THE LION WITHIN
5 Steps from Anger to Peace
RONDA CHERVIN

Help in Time of Need
ENCOURAGEMENT
PRACTICAL ADVICE
AND PRAYERS

En Route To Eternity

A Widow's Walk

See Appendix IV on page 177 for a full list with dates

Seeking Community

"Forgive us our trespasses, as we forgive those who trespass against us." (Mathew 6:12)

Looking back, I think the urge to try to find a "perfect community" within the wider community of the Church is partly because with my cultural Jewishness, I never fit in well in Catholic groups but still always craved community. Also, while I had trouble forgiving members of each group for whatever I didn't like about them, they also had trouble accepting my faults!

When a Catholic for a few years, I assumed that I would join a lay community surrounding the Von Hildebrands called the *Gemeinschaft* (German for "community"). They were all Benedictine Oblates as well. They came from different countries to a yearly retreat in Bavaria, Germany, and they met once a month with others in their own countries. Each one had a lay spiritual director in the community. Even though my German was rudimentary, I went to one such retreat and understood enough to want to become part of the group. However, when I went again later to this yearly retreat where the leaders would decide whether I could become a full member, I was told I didn't seem suited. I was flabbergasted and hurt. It took me awhile to understand their reason. There was a member at the retreat who was a writer. I had been told not to talk to him about his books, but not the reason why I shouldn't talk to him. Since I loved his books so much, I tried to persuade him to write another one. That was considered a sign of disobedience.

Maybe there were other reasons, too.

This happened just before I became a charismatic. I believe that God permitted this rejection to happen because I was meant to have a much more charismatic spirituality than their Benedictine one. There were several other lay communities I was attracted to, but I couldn't join because my husband hated groups. At one point, a famous spiritual director told me that I had absolutely the wrong personality for community life. Jesus once seemed to tell me: "You don't belong anywhere in the Church. I want to set you down in one place after another to teach for a while." More understanding of why I couldn't belong to a community came to me when reading a Vatican document about religious communities. All members must put love in the community above the apostolate. Now, I am always putting the apostolate of teaching Catholic truth above communal life. What do I mean? Take the example of the book of the *Gemeinschaft* writer I wanted to influence. The idea that his book could be an apostolic teaching tool was more important to me than obeying the head of the community.

On the positive side is my zeal for truth. On the negative, can you not detect a certain element of drama queen in this? Why wouldn't everyone in the community see me as a leader and want to do what would enhance my plans? Utopian fantasies are involved also. When I first meet a community or someone starting a group, I focus on everything wonderful about their rule and their personalities.

Now, none of the communities I tried – some 12 in 25 years – became a gulag! However, they all had inconsistencies and flawed personalities in them such that I was really better off as a consecrated woman on my own vs. as a member of that community. You would probably be interested in reading the pluses and minuses of each of these attempts. I do not want to satisfy your curiosity because that could fall under the sin of detraction. What is the sin of detraction? It's different from the sin of calumny. Calumny is when you tell lies about people to get them in trouble. Detraction is where what you say is true, but there is no compelling pastoral reason why others need to know these sad truths about others. So, instead of telling you about everything that caused me to leave one community after another, I will only give a sample of the virtues and problems of a few vaguely described groups.

One place was full of zeal and simplicity of life, but they were short on justice. I loved the passionate way the members wanted to convert the whole world. Simplicity of life has always attracted me. By that I mean not having luxuries when others have nothing. If one is not oneself poverty-stricken in the sense of destitution, by living with only necessities, we have much more to give to the poor. When challenged about this, many Catholics will cite instances where the charity one is asked to give to has executives on the board with a larger salary than the income of those of us who are asked to donate. To this I say, why not give to the Missionaries of Charity, the order founded by St. Mother Teresa of Calcutta, who feed the poorest of the poor, and who in India don't even have toilet paper!

Now, some of the communities I tried to join were really into simplicity of life. I loved watching one priest of such a community in the cafeteria. While others ate the good things in the bins in the cafeteria, he went to the fridge and took all the left-overs out and piled them pell-mell into his plate to eat! "In my stomach they are all mixed, so why not now?" he would respond when friends argued that these meals were yucky! However, the same group that was into such simplicity of life taught that instead of correcting injustices within the community that one member committed against another, it was better for the victim to offer it up as a penance. I couldn't accept this policy, so I left.

Here is one of theories about why others had less difficulty with such injustices and stayed in the community. My theory in hindsight is that community is similar to marriage in this respect. In many marriages in the honeymoon stage, we kind of idol-worship the spouse (Utopian?). Then after some years, the spouse can seem like a fallen idol. But if we forgive each other enough, we can see the spouse instead as a funny little creature and laugh at the same things that previously "drove us crazy." So, someone called to communal life could first see the community as an idol of perfection; then as a fallen idol, but with forgiveness and forbearance, as composed of members who have some virtues and some flaws. Instead of being unbearable to be with, they would be seen more as funny.

In another community I tried to join, the founder was warm, compassionate, and deeply contemplative, but a hoarder.

After years of trying out such groups, full of virtues but also with big flaws, a spiritual director suggested I should found my own community of consecrated widows. Guess what? When I was the drama queen running the utopia, the other potential members didn't like everything about me or my rules! So, becoming a consecrated widow seemed like a good answer. There is a movement in the Church to develop a rule of life and a ritual for consecrated widows. This was actually the first consecration in the Church. You can find in Acts descriptions of gossipy drunken widows, but also descriptions of those who didn't remarry and lived for Jesus and the Church. (For more about this, see my book *Walk With Me, Jesus: A Widow's Walk*.) The canonical rite for consecration of widows has not yet been worked out. In the meantime, bishops can experiment with it. I tried asking some bishops in places I was teaching if I could be such an experimental consecrated widow. No one seemed enthusiastic. One of my directors suggested that I become a dedicated widow with a private promise and my own rule of life. The rule I devised in 1999 includes daily Holy Mass, rosary, mercy chaplet, Office of Readings, Evening Prayer, Night prayer, and an hour of quiet prayer. I choose to wear second hand blue denim jumpers that I can buy cheaply so as to have more money to give to the poor. A few women followed me, each with her own rule of life. Of these, Marti Armstrong is the one I know the best. She is a grandmother, a pastoral counselor, a 3rd Order Franciscan, and very contemplative.

I believe my decision to become a dedicated widow is part of seeing God Alone as Enough!

The next chapter is about my work of writing and teaching and media presentation. In most of the places I have taught or lived, I tried joining communities in spite of previous failures. But, since my teaching and writing seemed much more graced, I am happy to move on to this next chapter in the latter years of my long life.

Teaching and Writing

"My heart cries out on a joyful theme...my tongue like the pen of the swiftest scribe." (Liturgy of the Hours)
"And to some the gift of teaching..." (Romans 12:7)

After my husband's death, I taught at many places and wrote many, many books.

Here is a list of the places I taught full time after I became a widow: Franciscan University of Steubenville, Notre Dame Apostolic Institute, St. John's Seminary of the Archdiocese of Los Angeles, Our Lady of Corpus Christi, and Holy Apostles College and Seminary. My teaching gift also came into play in giving conference talks, parish workshops, retreats, and interviews on EWTN Catholic TV and radio presentations.

Mother Angelica and I.

Whenever EWTN replays the series I did with Anne Lassiter about my book *The Widow's Walk,* I get emails from widows wanting more information about their options.

In this chapter, I would like to tell you about the key insights that went into these teachings as they can be found in my books. The gift of writing books began way back in 1969 when I began to teach. When I got my Ph.D. in philosophy at Fordham University in 1967, my twins were only 3 years old, and I hoped to have many, many, children. So, I thought of teaching as being something I might do on the side – maybe one course here and there. I thought I might write a scholarly article or two, as well. Sad miscarriages changed that plan. Humorously, my first such philosophy course was at an Army base in Southern California. There was a huge gun cemented onto the table. The students were so polite, partly because the captain of their squadron was attending the class!

When my husband's asthma was getting worse and worse, he urged me to look for a full-time teaching post. I was hired at Loyola Marymount University, partly because the chair was an admirer of Edith Stein, the Jewish convert phenomenologist and later a canonized saint. He thought I might be something like her. Besides, this was in 1969 when feminist pressure had resulted in attempts to have at least a token woman professor, especially in areas that are usually male, like philosophy departments! Because of John Paul II's letter on the *Dignity and Vocation of Woman*, written in 1988, even women teachers who previously had not considered themselves to be feminists began to call themselves Christian feminists.

One of the least known of such groups of women was called Feminists for Life. They pointed out that abortion favors those men who want sex without fatherhood, and the mostly male abortionists make most of the money. Having converted out of an atheist family background where abortion was considered an essential right of women, when I understood the truths of ethics, I became a fierce pro-life Catholic. My book, *Living in Love: About Christian Ethics*, includes a scenario of a couple of pre-meds in college who have to make a choice about abortion. I refute all their typical excuses such as "Everybody's doing it," "My conscience doesn't bother me," "It's for the greater good," "Nobody's perfect, I'm not a saint," etc. For 10 years, I joined others in the "Shield of Roses" who prayed in front of an abortion clinic in Los Angeles and offered help to those who thought they had no choice. Later, when teaching at Holy Apostles College and Seminary, I joined a group of the priests, faculty, sisters, and lay people praying in front of an abortuary in Connecticut. I was so in admiration of these Catholics going out in sometimes snowy, zero-degree weather.

In case any descriptions of my books in this chapter lead you want to find how to get a hold of them, you can find out how in the appendix of this book. Some of them are now free e-books on En Route Books and Media. This publisher took over many of my out-of-print books, as well as printing many new ones. Eventually, I would write some 65 small and large books. There is such a joy in seeing something published. It is just not the same as reading a manuscript, not only because of the wider range of readers, but just that a book is a certain kind of product that needs s certain way of being presented. About ten of my books are philosophical, one of the best being *Voyage to Insight*. I have always been so happy that some of my best students became teachers themselves. From my years at Loyola Marymount, Michael Healy and James Harold are now philosophy professors at Franciscan University of Steubenville. Kathy Hall Campitelli is an art teacher, influenced in her faith by my classes. Sister Xuan Pham, A Vietnamese Sister, loved my class on Way of Love, translated some of it into Vietnamese, and teaches it to other Sisters in Vietnam.

Very recently, I put on my blog on goodbooksmedia some pages with the title, TRANSFORMATIVE CATHOLIC PHILOSOPHY. Of the group of professors who participated, I want to mention by name Steve Bujno, who taught my book *Way of Love* to high school students and then wrote his own version called *A Way of Love* with examples even more suitable for teens.

The large majority of my books fall into the category of lay spirituality. In a certain sense, I have been promoting a philosophical type of spirituality. I analyze daily life situations as related to the concepts of the individuals involved, and then I show how grace can help. An example would be the one you have been reading about here – the "drama queen" analogy is based on a false concept of the self being the center of reality vs. making God central.

A philosophical book I wrote that I consider to be one of my best is *Feminine, Free and Faithful*. It came out of a course in Philosophy of Woman. The purpose is to show that women don't have to choose between traditional feminine traits and greater freedom if they are faithful to the Holy Spirit. In courses and parish workshops, I hand out a sheet that separates character traits into negative feminine traits (such as gossipiness and weakness); positive feminine traits (such as nurturing and compassion); negative masculine traits (such as cruelty and coldness); and positive masculine traits (such as leadership and strength).

Subsequent chapters lay out three theories of femininity and masculinity:

Complementarity: women and men were created to be different. If they try for the positive traits of the opposite sex, they wind up with the negative ones, and you have to deal with tough, cold women and effeminate, soft men.

Feminism: Men have been oppressing women throughout the centuries. They excuse this by caricaturing women with negative feminine traits. Women and men should be seen as equal in all ways.

Wholeness Theory: Women need to have all the positive masculine traits and men the positive feminine traits – so you can have women bankers and soldiers as well as male nurses and poets.

After critiquing these theories, my book presents what I consider to be the Christian philosophy of woman. Read it, you'll like it!

Sebastian Mahfood, of En Route Books and Media, has taken over my website recently. He calls my life-work by the title: Philosophical Spirituality.

Senbastian Mahfood and I.

How come I went from planning, to writing scholarly articles, to writing so many books? It started with this incident. I noticed that my first students didn't seem to like the books I assigned in the courses.

"What do you like to read?" I asked one day.

"Oh, Dr. Ronda, we don't like to read, we like to surf!"

I think it was from the Holy Spirit, to whom I prayed so much at charismatic prayer meetings, that I got the impulse to try writing a book they would like. My first attempt was *Church of Love*. It is an extended analogy of how people act when they are in love with Catholic practice. For example, if your boyfriend or girlfriend doesn't want to date on Saturday night, you think they probably have someone else they date. Now if in all the hours of the week we can't give an hour Sunday morning to Jesus at Holy Mass, there must be something we love more.

I xeroxed copies of *Church of Love* for the students and made ten more to send out to Catholic publishers. After nine rejection letters I forgot about it. But the tenth publisher, Liguori, not only published that one, but six more after that! Later, *Church of Love* went out of print. The Daughters of St. Paul (Pauline Books) made a booklet out of it called *Signs of Love*. That eventually also went out of print. Imagine my delighted surprise when I found that Magnificat, the monthly booklet of meditations, started excerpting the whole book.

These books were followed by four co-authored works with Sister Mary Neill, O.P. (A theology professor and spiritual director). Maybe because I am a twin, I simply love co-authoring books. *A Woman's Tale, Bringing the Mother With you (Healing Meditations of the Mysteries of the Rosary), Finding the Father (about the Our Father)*, and *Great Saints, Great Friends* are all books blending insights from theology, philosophy, and Christian psychology.

Here is a photo of Sister Mary Neill, O.P. and myself.

Sister Mary Neill, OP, and myself.

Other wonderful co-authors I have partnered with include Lois Janis, Ross Porter, Terri Vorndran, Don Briel, Eileen Spotts, Gene Grandy, Msgr. Joseph Pollard, Fr. Eugene Kevane, Carla Conley, Ruth and Richard Ballard, Sebastian Mahfood, Kathleen Brouillette, and Al Hughes. And, of course, all those who contributed chapters to my anthologies. See Appendix for my Books by Date.

My first public speaking engagement was for a conference of Catholic United for the Faith. I was pretty frightened. A colleague of mine took me aside with this advice: "Don't be afraid of being a show-off when you speak. Most people hate public speaking, God can only use show-offs to speak for Him." Later, I did many talks at Charismatic Conferences and then started giving parish workshops and retreats. These usually came out of books I wrote to respond to some need in my students or in the wider Church. Obvious examples would be writing books about widow saints to help widows; books about traumas such as rejection, or grieving.

One of my all-time favorite books I wrote is called *Taming the Lion Within: 5 Steps from Anger to Peace.* It came out of a challenge from a spiritual director.

"Ronda, I can keep absolving you from sins of anger, but why don't you try to get at the psychological root of all that rage?"

This was just before I went to teach at Franciscan University. In the corridors of that fine place, a graduate student handed me a flyer, asking me to pass it around: **ARE YOU PLAGUED BY ANGER, FEAR,**

or DEPRESSION? Come to weekly meetings to find out how to overcome these blights... I immediately thought: "Here is my chance to deal better with anger." Thus began my experience with Recovery, International – started in the United States before 12 Steps of the same name, Recovery, was founded in the 1940's by Dr. Abraham Low, a Jewish psychiatrist. Low noticed that he could help patients in the hospital, but when they went home, they couldn't handle ordinary life. The self-help methods he devised grew from once-a-week meetings in Chicago to an organization that spans the whole world! I was part of these meetings as a member or as a leader for 20 years. At the meetings, the participants talk about applying certain concepts to their problems. One of these so-called tools is called "averageness vs. exceptionality." It helped me with the "drama queen" syndrome.

Here is a typical sharing of mine regarding this concept.

Ronda: "I didn't get such a great evaluation from the students in one of my classes this semester. I feel like a failure."

Another member: "If the average is "C," why would a "B" rating be a failure?"

Leader: It is exceptionality to think that we have to be super-terrific in order to be good at something. Abraham Low teaches that we should hope to be average. Then we can feel glad if we are above average in some endeavor, but we only set ourselves up for anxiety, anger, and depression if we project in the future an exceptional success. Come to think of it, dear reader, I would feel "exceptionally" happy, if even one of you decides to look into Recovery, International (free, by donation, in face-to-face groups, but also by phone or email) because of reading this page!

Now, after Recovery, International helped me a lot, I would talk it up in classes and in parishes. However, I noticed that many Catholics are allergic to anything psychological. They think of such programs as a danger to their faith. So, the Holy Spirit inspired me to write a book combining the insights of Abraham Low with Catholic spirituality.Voila! *Taming the Lion Within: 5 Steps from Anger to Peace.* My daughters, both tech experts, wrote a Facilitator's Guide for others to use in teaching it. It can be found with the book *Taming the Lion* at the En Route Books website.

This may be a good place to mention all the help I have gotten along my journey from psychological counseling – some being Catholic therapists but one Jewish, and one even an atheist. Thank you, God, for using these counselors to help me. As is the case with all my excellent spiritual directors, I am not mentioning names of most of these counselors or directors. Some have left this earth. Others are winding down rather than looking for more "customers!"

In another vein, I find what is derisively called Pop Psychology to be important to me in understanding my own patterns of behavior, and especially those of others. For example, instead of being frustrated with introverts who don't want to tell me everything they are thinking, I say to myself: "It is as hard for 'x' to open himself up verbally as it is for me to keep anything quiet!" Because as mentioned above, so many Catholics will have nothing to do with psychology, I wrote an article recently explaining my perspective. You can find it in the Appendix.

As I am writing this chapter of *Further Along the Road*, it occurs to me that God's Providence has found a way to "redeem" my drama queen tendencies by means of teaching, speaking, and writing in this way. Students who love my classes, not all of course, and those who hear me speak, often say that what they like best about me is my "transparency." "Dr. Ronda, when you give all these personal examples of the truths you are teaching, even about vulnerable stuff, it is easier for me to relate the remedies to my own life-story, especially in areas where my problems are kind of secret." Now, only drama queens are willing to tell awful things about their lives just because it makes for "a good story." How about the "Every utopia becomes a gulag" issue? The tendency to look toward a perfect outcome, so unrealistic and toxic in family life and in communities, takes a different form in teaching and writing.

Why?

Because it is part of the mission of teaching philosophy and spirituality to tell listeners about ideals.

Example: I am telling retreatants or a Catholic TV audience about different types of love in C.S. Lewis' *Four Loves*. They need to hear that beautiful side of family love – what it can be. If they only hear about the problems, they can give up, as have many people in our times who are afraid to marry and have families. After they grasp the ideal, then I give them ideas that will help them to deal with the prob-

The Ridley family.

lems. One of my most amusing memories of my dear son is about his idea of my profession. When eight years old, he was asked in school to write about the occupations of his parents, and he came up with the following: "My mother is a small, fierce philosopher!"

It was thrilling to be invited to speak in other countries. I was invited to Germany to give a retreat to the US military wives. I spoke twice in Australia and once in Canada. You can find about ten years of chatty daily insights of mine on a blog on James Ridley's website: goodbooksmedia.

Because I got an M.A. in spirituality at Notre Dame Institute while teaching philosophy there during several summers, I got to occasionally teach introduction to spirituality at Holy Apostles Seminary. While there, I put together with Kathleen Brouillette, a parish minister, a book called *"Spirituality for All Times: Excerpts from the Classics."* It has ten pages each of the great writings of our tradition. Students love getting a taste for St. Augustine, St. Benedict, St. Gertrude, St. Francis, St. Bernard, St. Ignatius, St. Teresa of Avila, St. John of the Cross, and many more. Of course, all these writers believe that "God Alone is Enough!"

I think you can easily guess the contents of some of the other books I have written by scanning the Appendix at the end of this book. I believe that of all the books I have written in the last twenty-five years, *The Way of Love* is the most useful. It is an inexpensive compilation of four shorter books, three of them coming right out of parish ministry opportunities.

- What is Love?
- Overcoming Obstacles to Love
- Living in Love: About Christian Ethics (described above)
- The Way of Love: Step by Step

I especially enjoy challenging readers with new ideas about types of love, ways to overcome such common obstacles to love as anxiety, bossiness, non-forgiveness, etc.

One of my favorite shocking challenges is this: If you asked family, friends, colleagues, and parishioners what your worst character trait is, you might find that they all agree, and you are surprised! But the challenge that reader/participants find the most helpful is extremely easy to do. It consists of spending a whole week thanking God for everything good in one's life – not just huge things like the beauty of the sky, but tiny things like having toilet paper or salt. Try it, you'll be surprised how happy this makes you!

Another favorite that came out of teaching in seminaries is *Last Call: 12 Men who Dared Answer – Stories of Late Vocations to the Priesthood.* We have such a shortage of priests. Many older men would be fine priests, but they think they are unworthy to even try. After reading the stories written by these late vocation men, they take hope.

Books I wrote about aging, about hoping for heaven, and problems of Catholics in their 70's and 80's will be cited in the last chapter of *Further Along the Road.*

Also! How could I forget to mention my novels?

I was brought up by a mother who read a novel a week, if not more. I have always loved fiction, especially reading about drama queens such as Scarlett O'Hara or Anna Karenina. It wouldn't take a rocket scientist to guess that eventually after publishers became interested in my non-fiction books, I would want to write a novel. I did write one. In fact, I wrote five: *Ties that Bind, A Summer Knight's Tale* with co-author Gene Grandy, *Last Fling*, and two with pseudonyms you might never find! I'm not telling! I loved writing the novels. *Ties that Bind* was about a married couple in trouble, with dual chapters about the same events – one from the standpoint of the wife; the other from the perspective of the husband. *A Summer Knight's Tale* was about a far-out (utopia-minded?) priest who gets into messes because he is so idealistic. *Last Fling* is about the heroine of *Ties that Bind* after she becomes a widow. These were all privately printed while I sought a publisher. Even though I never found one, friends who read them like them a lot. Check them out in the Appendix.

Golly, gee, how about this chapter for manifesting a gift for PR! Smile.

Literary Works 2004 to Present

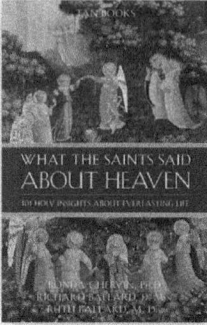

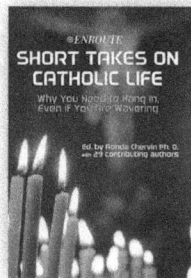

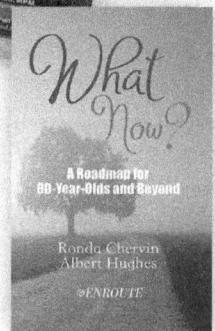

*See Appendix IV on page 177
for a full list with dates*

Journal Excerpts (1998 - 2002)

"What else have I in heaven but you?
Apart from you I want nothing on earth.
My body and heart faint for joy.
God is my possession forever...
To be near God is my happiness.
I have made the Lord God my refuge." (Psalm 73)

"Put on, as God's chosen ones, holy and beloved, heartfelt compassion, kindness, humility, gentleness and patience, bearing with one another and forgiving one another. If one has a grievance against another; as the Lord has forgiven you, so must you do also and over all these put on love, that is, the bond of perfection and let the peace of Christ control your hearts, the peace into which you are also called in one body." (Colossians 3: 12-17)

The journals from which I have excerpted here are the fruits of contemplative prayer. As described earlier in my chapter on my consecration, my prayer life has always included a contemplative dimension.

A few distinctions:

- **Prayer of petition** – asking God for particular favors for self or others.

- **Meditation** – reading spiritual books, especially the Bible, and pondering what those words and images could mean for one's own journey.

- **Contemplation** – where there are few words and the mind, heart, and soul open themselves to truths, feelings, and aspirations inspired by God at God's initiative.

Now a Catholic contemplative is a person whose prayer life, besides Holy Mass and formal Liturgy of the Hours and other prayers with fixed words, is characterized by such words and images of supernatural origin. As explained earlier, that does not mean that all contemplatives are saints. Someone could have all sorts of words and images coming directly from evil spirits! One spiritual director of mine told me that I was not a contemplative, but was rather an extremely active person with contemplative graces. I feel especially graced when a contemplative befriends me. The three friends who fall into this category the most are Charles Rich, Fr. Gregory Elmer, O.S.B., and Gary McCabe. Charles Rich, I told you about earlier. Fr. Gregory was a monk at St. Andrew's Abbey in Valyermo, California. He sometimes gave me private retreats. How about this advice he once gave me, since without using those words, he certainly detected my drama queen side:

"Melodrama, you know, Ronda, is the theatre of the ego. Making scenes is a way to escape from the long hard work of crucified love called patience. Benedictine monks are to share in the sufferings of Christ by patience. When you are agitated, cultivate solitude. This is good because there is no one to play-act before when you are alone."

The third contemplative I have known well is Gary McCabe, a family man, earlier immersed in the world of business, who is now a retired single living in the world but leading a contemplative prayer life. Most influenced by the spirituality of St. Ignatius of Loyola, he spends hours in Adoration lifting his heart and the hearts of all those he loves to God. He gives private retreats based on the famous 30-Day Retreats of Ignatius. I consider one moment of deep surrender in contemplative prayer worth any book I have written. Think about it, is heaven going to be projects or contemplation? We need to prepare now.

So, even though I am not a contemplative as a vocation, I want to share with you the best thoughts I received in the contemplative part of my own prayer life in the last 25 years. These often come during the half-hour-and-hour times of silent prayer that are part of my daily life as a Dedicated Widow. But they also come unexpectedly, even in noisy places like airports, or wake me in the night. I am excerpting these from a book of journals I called *6 Toes in Eternity* which can be found on the website of En Route Books and Media. Now, this book of journal writings includes many details of my life at various teaching institutions and parishes. It also has comments about the problems of the Church during these times. I want this chapter, however, not to be about those many incidents and issues, however interesting, but about the highlights of the way I heard Jesus speaking to me over these years. Most of my selections are words I thought were from Jesus, but sometimes I include my own thoughts or those of others because I have the feeling they will be helpful to you, my dear readers.

My prayer: Dear Jesus, Mary, and Joseph, and widow saints, I truly believe that you want me to select excerpts from these many writings to be available for others to read. But I am a little afraid. I don't want my "drama queen tendencies" to permeate this book. Instead I want it to be a form of heaving up my mind, heart, and soul to you, holy family, that you may heal me of wounds of the past, and bring hope to readers struggling with similar difficulties.

June 13, 1998 (at an airport):

I had a sense of my soul leaving my body and total unification with God. I no longer want insights about God, only God himself. This reminded me of the famous spiritual book called *The Cloud of Unknowing*, written for those who long for wordless prayer.

Dressing almost like a nun in my drab blue dresses and jumpers feels like being covered, hidden. Instead of my clothing being self-expression through exterior wrappings, my true self lives within. I no longer display myself in time, but instead invisibly stretch myself toward eternity.

(The excerpts in the next pages are from my time at Our Lady of Corpus Christi College.)

November 15, 2001

I had an interior vision while sitting in the chapel in Adoration. It was of that face of El Greco's Christ on the Veil of Veronica that was part of my spiritual marriage. The words I heard him speaking in my heart as I looked at that Spanish face were those of St. Bernard: "Love is not Loved!"

When I stared into your sad El Greco eyes, my Jesus, those words "Love is not Loved!" came to me not as a general statement but as directed by You to me. It seems that You wanted me to know just how wounding it is for You that I will not trust the love that You went to such lengths to prove to me. Staring at the pure whiteness of Your presence in the host in the monstrance, and then down at Your face in the painting, I tried to respond.

I could produce many reasons why I don't love Love enough:

Is it easier for me to love you as truth

because truth is strong and love is vulnerable?

Is it easier for me to love you as beauty

because beauty is sublime and love is messy?

Is it easier for me to love you as mercy

because mercy is balm and love is strenuous?

When I look into Your tragic eyes, my Jesus, I think the reason might be deeper still. Terror of surrender to Your Divine heart whose beat is so loud I could no longer hear my own? Fear that after diving into Your waves You might cast me out on the shore even more helpless to survive?

Or still more simply, that I could refuse You nothing, no matter how painful, if I was close enough to know You wanted it!

I hear You telling me that I cannot experience the fullness of Your love for me if I am afraid to come closer. "Perfect love casts out fear." Surrender!

Yet a perfect unison of heartbeat with Jesus would render me more like you, Mother Mary. You certainly did not emerge from your surrender to the Holy Spirit as a dead fish. No! Rather as Queen of Apostles!

November 15, 2001: evening:

I had a visit with a couple I hoped to become friends with: Michael and Francette Meaney. It was a wonderful time. Afterwards, Jesus seemed to admonish me in a sweet way. "I told you that if you would be mine, you would also get the human love you needed. Why such surprise that I came through?" And now I am thinking about that. Is it true? Will it ever be enough, my Jesus, to belong simply to You? Of course, I will always also need human friends, but will I always be seeking human closeness with such desperation?

You seem to reply that You want me to seek human love, for my sake and for the sake of those who can benefit by my love in return, no matter how flawed. I do not need to love humans less. I need to love You more. In that way I can come to others with more tenderness than thirst. That terrible thirst will have been quenched by Your love. You remind me that if I will "be still and know that You are God," I will be less anxious and fretful.

I have often had an image of God stretching us like a rubber band way beyond the size we would like to be. Is that so we can encircle more of reality? In any case, I see in my mind's eye an image of You on a secure throne beckoning me to come into Your lap and let You hold me tight against all those fears, irrational and legitimate. Will I take the time to sit with You until Your "perfect love can cast out all fear"?

November 16, 2001

I was talking to Jesus about a tendency I see for us to so imagine You as a Jew of Your time on earth that we don't realize you encompass all nationalities in your understanding and love. You seemed to say:

"I was incarnate as Jesus of Nazareth in time in a manner that would make it possible for the most people to follow Me. Yet all beauty, goodness, and truth are in My divine nature."

Saturday, November 17, 2001

Jesus seemed to tell me that I am always trying to leap above the cross of fear of rejection with wings of insight. It just postpones the pain till the next loss. Instead, He made me realize that He wants me to plunge into His heart to unite my pain with His and Mother Mary's. Then He can bring me closer to You who bring a comfort that no intellectual understanding can bring. Face to face means heart to heart.

November 21, 2001

Here is a beautiful quotation I read from the poet George Herbert: "Love is the liquor sweet and most divine, which my God feels as blood; but I, as wine."

November 26, 2001

Today we had a groundbreaking for our new chapel. It was cold and windy but glorious to see representatives of so many groups who love our school come out for the Bishop's blessing.

I hear Mary, Mother of the Church, speaking in my heart. "Dearest daughter, take the time to ponder deeply these sublime moments where everything comes out even better than you could hope. It is true that you are too physically weak for ascetical sacrifices, but I do want you to accept small discomforts such as the cold and the wind tonight so that you will be free to enjoy times like these, full of grace. I want to be for you like a mother encouraging a small, whiny child. When you feel bent out of shape, take my hand and let me mother you through the tiny difficulties of daily life."

November 27, 2001

We read in biographies that you, St. Teresa of Avila, sometimes watched the hands turning on the clock and sighed, "One minute less of this tedious life before entering the joys of eternity."

I hear Teresa of Avila laughing at me. She seemed to say that nothing is perfect outside of heaven. I imagine Teresa chiding me, "Be less rigid, Ronda. If I amused the nuns when they were bored by dancing with castanets, find your own way to get out of whatever bad moods the devil wants to throw you into."

When I question the relative "messiness" of the way our community lives, might God want to remind me that if He preferred uniformity to variety, He would never have created hippos as well as stallions? And aren't I, myself, more like a hippo than a stallion?

December 11, 2001

I read a poem by Daniel Varholy, a faculty member here at Our Lady of Corpus Christi, dedicated to you, Holy Spirit. These lines were the most provocative or moving for me:

"Forgetting You is our greatest sin of omission..."

"We ache for you when we are anxious..."

"We pity our solitude, painting and embroidering sorrows..."

"Out of forgettings, doubts and faithless denials..."

"And yet You are there, suspended in the gentleness of holy composure..."

"O let us remember with each heart's motion, your holiest beating

Of wings and breath enabling our hearts to be hearts of flesh."

I was praying to Mary about my conflicts with authority figures. She seemed to say that she didn't have a juridical role in the early Church. She was mother. I need to follow her by being a motherly widow at the college, not in an authority role except in the classroom.

December 22, 2001

Jesus, You remind me of Your image of many mansions. You chide me for being too philosophical in the sense of always wanting unity, such as everything should be equal and the same, instead of appreciating the astounding variety of creatures and ways of being You have made. Even heaven will not be sheer oneness. I will be one with You, Jesus, but also united in a different way with whomever and whatever You choose to make my heaven. "Be still and know that I am God," You tell me as I struggle so fruitlessly to try to fit everything into my own brain.

St. Joseph, I don't have a clear image of you. The best comes from the Zeffirelli film, Jesus of Nazareth, because he makes you so Jewish, but we don't see you in that film when you were older.

St. Joseph, you seem to answer that you would like to be my father now spiritually. I could try praying to you not only for practical problems and family crises but also just heart to heart.

Yes!

December 23, 2001

Jesus, Mary, Joseph, how complex we are! I still feel uncomfortable in any Church, including St. Peter's, that is highly embellished. A whole village scene nativity such as is found in the Churches of Italy delights me even though it is hardly simple, because it is folk-art. For myself, I cannot bear to buy anything I don't need when that money could be given to the starving.

When I turn to You, my Jesus, for confirmation of my artistic tastes, you always tell me that even if simplicity is better in terms of asceticism and giving everything unneeded to the poor, you honor the intent of those who adorn your Church with gold and gems. Their desire is to give to You the very best, no matter what the cost.

(This segment is a little longer because I think you need more of a context to understand the final seeming words from Mother Mary.)

My twin sister, Carla De Sola Eaton, a sacred dancer, appeared on the cover of the oldest, most well-known magazine of the dance world: DANCE. A copy arrived today. The photo was of herself, swathed like a nun, in the role of Mary at the crucifixion.

Oh, dear Mother Mary, how happy I am that it was in this pose and costume that she appeared to thousands of readers. You are one of the bonds between us.

Liturgical dance has a long history of acceptance in ages past, but has faced rejection in our times, especially by the U.S. Bishops. For centuries, dance was connected to feast days in the Catholic Church, some dances even devised for the Bishop. Today, in countries such as those in Africa, dance is a completely integrated part of liturgical processions. And these dances are demonstrated with pride at Papal visits. In the United States, sacred dance began in New York City on the steps of Churches as choreographed by my sister, and a group formed around her. Quickly taken up by post-Vatican II liturgical innovators, it spread throughout the country. My sister's company, Omega, dances with incredible beauty, and never in a way to stimulate any kind of unchaste thoughts in the congregation.

Unfortunately, other liturgical dancers of less professional ability or discernment have managed to offend congregations with tight costumes and gestures more associated at times with popular dance motifs than the modern dance or ballet style of the originators. This led to a ruling against all dance in the liturgy, which was followed by the obedient but defied by those who weren't inclined to obey anything coming from the Bishops or the Vatican, if it was contrary to their own ideas.

A happy compromise came about with the use of the term *sacred dance* to include concerts and private prayer outside the Mass, and liturgical dance was done within church services. My sister and her company do both liturgical dance and sacred dance. Since Carla's dances are sublime and of an ineffable spiritual inspiration, I find myself defending what she is doing to the maximum, while deploring any dance at Mass or in concert that is truly distracting. Hopefully, the many beautiful sacred dancers who conduct courses and workshops will eventually elevate this art to such a peak that no one will be able to object.

I turn to you now, dear Mary. You come from a Jewish culture where movement, not stillness, was the rule in public worship. Did you like to see twentieth century charismatics adding swaying and raised hands to the liturgy of your son's sacrifice? Did you understand the motives of professional sacred dancers as well?

I imagine you replying that you rejoice in all praise of your Son. I picture you loving rapt stillness for yourself and other Christians, but also loving ecstatic joyful physical expression. You also tell me that it saddens you if men and women are distracted from the Mass, itself a kind of ritual dance, when performers move in such a manner that can lead to sensual images in the minds of the onlookers or participants.

I seem to hear you in my heart asking me not to analyze the matter to death but instead to pray that in anticipation of the resurrected body in heaven we will all someday be united in both absorbed stillness and full bodily worship.

Here is a photo of me and my sister Carla in our 70s with Father Phillip of St. Andrew's Abbey:

December 27, 2001

I listened today to Vaughn Williams' Mass in G. It is celestial. I was reminded again of Cardinal Newman's famous observation that in the greatest music we are overhearing the angels singing in heaven. If this is true, may I thank all ye angels for the many concerts you share with us here on earth?

January 1, 2002

Holy Mary, exalted widow, even though "old" in your days was much younger than in ours, I imagine you have a special place in your heart for older people. How happy you are to see us availing ourselves of the comfort of your Son, the only source of enduring solace for any person.

January 2, 2002

At a family visit full of good cheer and good food, I thought:

If I think of you, married women saints, I can imagine you putting in plenty of effort and loving attention on your wifely duties, but not investing as much personal pride in the matter as to be devastated by small failures. Teach us, dear saints, how to balance loving conscientiousness in serving with a lightness of touch. As soon as we invest too much ego in all of this, our tension takes away from the conviviality that should come in family fellowship when there is plenty of mutual forgiveness in the mix.

January 3, 2002

One of the intercessory prayers at Mass today was, "Help families to come into a greater love of one another." There is so much love in my family now, thanks be to God. Much more harmony.

Holy Family, I think you rejoice to see love between your children. I sometimes picture you, together, Jesus, Mary, and Joseph, looking down on earth – heads close together, excited each time you see love instead of indifference or hate. Wouldn't you have shared such observation of good in your family setting in Nazareth?

The Holy Father's (Pope Benedict's) New Year's message included these words: "There can be no peace without justice, and no justice without forgiveness." He wrote that forgiveness seems like a short-term loss, like weakness. It demands great strength and spiritual courage both in the granting it and in accepting it. To how many situations in my life could I apply these words of Christian wisdom!

But my Jesus, how often even with forgiveness there is no justice. Then what? You reply, then there is no peace in the sense of feelings of equilibrium. But there is always redemptive suffering. You don't have to pretend it's all fine. Some will be called to inner peace in spite of the exterior conflict. Others will be called to fight harder for justice. Others, who can, will have to leave those situations to find either kind of peace.

How do I know which response You want from me?

You seem to reply, "I want inner peace for everyone. If you can't find it in unjust situations through offering the suffering or through fighting harder, and I give you a way out, I will be not be sad or angry if you take it."

January 7, 2002

A poem of John Paul II helps me with accepting terrible things that happen. The verses come out of the Pope's time working in a quarry lifting heavy rocks during World War II.

"When I bare an equal weight of horror and hope

then no one will accuse me of simplicity."

I think he means by the second line that doubters of the faith tend to brand believers as naïve. That impression can rarely be erased by anything short of heroic suffering. So, my Father in heaven, show me how to follow the lead of the head of your Church – to suffer but not to doubt.

January 9, 2002

A funny thing: I was visiting a friend who is a nurse. When she noticed I was aimlessly poking my crochet needle into my ear she screamed her outrage. "You could break an eardrum, you idiot, use a Q-tip!" The sorrowful part was in explaining why I don't use Q-tips. Just before my husband's death, he bought at a discount at Sam's Club some three thousand Q-tips. It took me about five years to use them up, always with a sense of the loss of him accompanying the loss of whatever was plugging my ears! As a result, I hate them now.

Most widows talk about the way the oddest things become symbols of the previous presence of the spouse, and now of the lack of that presence. I find it even harder to listen to cello music since my dead son was a cellist. I hear Mother Mary scolding me for tossing off these last three paragraphs as if it was all comic. "Just lay your head in my lap, Ronda, and tell me how it feels not to have a husband, a best friend nearby always, and a son who is as far away as eternity." Yes, Mother Mary, in some vague way I realize you missed St. Joseph, the only one who knew the day by day revelation of the identity of your Son. And you missed Jesus when he ascended. He was both son and best friend to you as well as Savior and God. You want me to feel my loneliness and also to empathize with my daughters who miss Martin as father and Charlie as brother. They have wonderful husbands, but that doesn't mean there isn't a hole in their hearts.

Mary comforts, "When you feel that loneliness call on me. Am I not your mother?" And she adds, "Don't be afraid to yearn for Martin and Charlie and picture that great reunion, partly mediated by your faithful prayers for them. Do you think they are not in my arms because they might be in purgatory? Do you think that I am not in purgatory?"

(This locution was "confirmed" by a priest who mentioned in a sermon that there is a belief by some that Mary visits purgatory every first Saturday to bring some out with her!)

January 12, 2002

The response to the talks was different this time. Instead of coming up to tell me that they liked what I said, people said "I love *you!*" Others started giving me their possessions – a splendid wheeled backpack for my trip back, and old used candles! By the evening, the exhaustion was total. With tears in my throat I kept muttering "I can't do this anymore. I can't. I can't. I can't."

When I look into the sad eyes of the El Greco version of Your face, Jesus, I seem to feel You affirming me for the sacrifices of the past in giving conference talks, giving me permission to stop, but still glad if I keep going sometimes out of love for our poor Church.

January 15, 2002

I was thinking about how many of us where I teach seek holiness, openly and sometimes almost desperately. How much easier to feign mediocrity of intent so that the gap between wish and reality would not be so obvious and beckoning of critique!

Here I am, Jesus, your failure. But, no matter what, never let me set my sights so low that I cannot fail.

January 16, 2002

More talk that one of my closest friends in the Society is transferring from the college to another site soon. Grief and insecurity. I invest a lot in friendship, so the pain is greater at their loss than those who specialize in acquaintanceship. Do they do so precisely to avoid pain? Probably.

Jesus, you tell me that there is no way to avoid the cross, but crosses coming from love are the best. Would I rather have fewer friends?

January 18, 2002

A student who is discerning a vocation to the priesthood was telling some of us of his fear that in spite of the prospect of a well-paying job in the summer, he would not have enough money next year for tuition and expenses. I said I would give him a scholarship. He was so overwhelmed that he suddenly grabbed my hand and kissed it. (Later, he didn't need it.)

What joy that just by living simply, I can afford to give money when it is needed. Thank you, Father God, for giving me the talents and health to have earned a good living in the past, doing a job I love, and now I have a pension plus social security.

My dear friend Jeannie Hughes made a comment today that rings true. She said that people who complain a lot feel unloved. Since I am an expert "kvetch" – that's Yiddish for complainer – I pondered her remark carefully. Do I think that things would go smoothly if only everyone loved me more? In some ways that is probably true.

What bothers me no end is where there really is a way to make things better, but it is not done because the key persons appear, perhaps, just not to care enough. Someday, with your grace, Father, I will be able to take such disappointments lightly because faith in my own ascent someday to heaven will be greater. Would engaged couples resent small difficulties since their minds are floating in the bliss of the soon consummation of their greatest desire?

It seemed that the first person of the Trinity replied, "So, I'm not a good enough Father for you?"

January 20, 2002

Dear God, how is it possible that You have showered so many gifts on me, and I am yet such a wretched, desperate woman? The response I hear in my heart is that it doesn't matter how old we are, but what counts is that by the time of our deaths, we are full of gratitude for Your mercy and full of love for everyone, even those who have hurt us most.

January 22, 2002

Today is the grim anniversary of Roe vs. Wade. After dinner we went to a Mass at the cathedral in commemoration of the infant martyrs. I grieve for them, and for their parents with all the previous disordered choices they made that finally made that worst choice seem inevitable. Also, I feel shame for our country that we, who fought so hard against Nazi and Communist atrocities, should now be killing our own babies in the millions.

Lord, how long? Too little family love, too little virtue, too little hope?

January 23, 2002

Watching one of our black priests raising the Eucharistic Host up at the consecration today at Mass, I had a new thought. In the early Church, Africans were among the priests. I believe the most well-known country would be what is now Ethiopia. But here in the United States, how many years did You long to see black hands holding You up at the consecration?

January 24, 2002

Today was a red-letter day because I made contact with the representative who will process my social security payments to begin April 24th. I have been getting widow social security but due to my husband's disability, his amount was about half what mine will be. The glorious part was that the social security representative turned out to be a strong Christian. We had a fine conversation, and she accepted my offer to send her one of my books as a gift.

Dear Father God, those of us raised by parents who lived through the depression know better than younger ones what a change that initiative made in the lives of lower and middle-class people. Never again the need to save desperately for one's elderly years, or the specter of starvation. Thank you for inspiring those in government to devise this plan, however faulty in some respects. True, few middle-class people can live on social security alone in a style they are accustomed to. It is my theory, possibly flawed since my needs are different than those of others, that living in a large house with an empty nest is not necessarily so desirable for older people. I would prefer to see us in studio apartments surrounding a common area for fellowship. In Your providence, God of love, please help us to find ways to overcome the terrible loneliness of so many in our present-day culture.

One of my greatest wishes came through today for someone with whom I have been in conflict. I was glad of the spontaneous joy in my heart to see him so happy. Later in the same day, I got to enjoy seeing him having fun playing a game. That activity is not one I participate in, so it was particularly evident that my delight was for him. Since I am poor indeed when it comes to forgiveness of those whom I see as obstacles to my goals, I think this is a way that you are leading me into greater solidarity with such persons. If I was totally locked into seeing them as enemies, how could I rejoice for them?

January 26, 2002

I woke up to the Holy Spirit saying I would be less burdened if I didn't live so much in the future. O, "Be still and know that I am God." Help me, dear God, to slow down and savor what You give me in each moment.

January 28, 2002

Suddenly laughing in the midst of heavy conversation about problems at our school. What is that laugh? Hopeless, helpless, and feeling that it doesn't really matter so much, after all; that the wink of mirth in an eye maybe weighs more?

St. Philip Neri, you, such a humorous saint, help us to laugh!

January 29, 2002:

I told my class of my joy in their positive evaluations of the class since it proves that I can teach people their age. I need to accept that they are not so expressive as I am in their body language in class. Are they trying to be cool? Can I forgive them for that? They are still awkward. I need to have more compassion for them.

January 30, 2002

A holy young Sister asked during spiritual exercises: "Do we want to be a community of martyrs or of marshmallows?"

February 8, 2002

Claudel: "Jesus does not come to take away or explain suffering but to be present to it."

February 11, 2002

I have some wonderful friends here in Corpus Christi: The Ridley's. Claire and Jim. Claire wrote some thoughts:

"The tabernacle is small but holds all eternity.

I want to shrink to fit in there –

I want to be so small I could be held

In someone's palm and not be recognized.

I could get lost in the ciborium and tossed onto a paten –

Chosen out of all the other hosts

Not because I was so much more

Delectable but because I was

Utterly undetectable.

An indistinct wafer consumed by love of God."

February 13, 2002

So sad, always, to participate in our prayer in front of the abortion clinic! So many years of this peaceful protest.

(Note to readers: eventually every abortion clinic in Corpus Christi closed!)

February 14, 2002

My daughter Carla's Ash Wednesday Poem

(such a poignant description of what lapsed Catholics feel)

Mountaineer

Here's the hollow made to hold my head
When I was giant also, where I slept
before I left you. Here's the place I wept
The day I started shrinking when I fled.

I wonder, can you feel my thread-thin feet
Come skitter where my head once rested? I
Am just another ant who wonders why
You never chased me. Pointless to retreat.

I'm prodigal: at least, I've slept with swine.
But nothing works, not logic, loss of pride,
Nor climbing back despite the dark inside,
Annihilating darkness, undefined.

I hope. It happens sometimes that I grow
For minutes, even hours. Then I stride
Uphill on legs of light you may provide.
At any rate, I hope but cannot know.

At times, I sneak the trodden path instead,
Behind both light and darkness, tiny limbs
Beneath a premise bowed, a beast of whim.
I find this nook again. I rest my head.

February 15, 2002

Jesus, You seemed to ask at Holy Communion: "Why not concentrate on holiness vs. setting new deadlines?"

(The reference here is to a bad habit I have of setting artificial deadlines and then getting tense meeting them, as in, "I will finish this new book I am writing by April 10th," but the deadline is not required since the book will not be taught by me until September.)

February 16, 2002

At the Retreat Center where I went to live, still teaching some days each week at the college.

Anne Lassiter, a nurse, now a Catholic widow and a TV crusader for the faith, lives in a house at the Retreat Center. She has the kind of goodness I like in women – not too sweet, weak, or smothering. She is somehow vulnerable but gutsy and humble, needy but not hysterical. I am trying to take it very slow because I need such a friend at this point.

Glorious Mystery:

Here at the Center, I felt such a longing to be in the chapel in the middle of the day. Jesus seemed to say, "Curl up like a snail in the shell that is My embrace, my poor, tired little old bride. Rest! A bride is all openness and warmth; not tense work mode."

You seem to tell me to offer Your grace to staunch the wounds of priests who have lost the desire to meet You in the Mass every day. I made the image into a little poem:

Lick the bloody dust of the via dolorosa

Staunch the incurable wounds of My priests

Not with stinging taunts

Rather with a Mary-kiss of compassionate love.

February 17, 2002

Joyful Mystery:

The topic of discipline came up. Discipline is so needed, but not too tight! Otherwise, without discipline, with just pure laxity, people wind up like Oblomov (the famous "hero" of a Russian satire). The Holy Spirit seemed to say that we must be transformed by love, not just to avoid laziness and disorder, but so that we do more out of love.

February 18, 2002

Quiet peace at Adoration, and revival of carefree mood – Office of Readings: Exodus, "You were the slaves to Egypt but I will take you as my own people." I am a slave to workaholism. God wants to free me to become slower and more serene.

A Sister I respect at the college said that to be proud, impatient, and judgmental are three vices of converts!

February 19, 2002

Rabbi Zolli, the famous head rabbi of Rome who converted partly under the influence of Pius XII, in his book about Jesus says that Jesus would have sung his sermons!

February 20, 2002

Suppose purgatory is when I get to feel what my victims did when I was hurting them, but then they forgive me and they get to feel what they did and I forgive them? Total healing of memories. It would then expand the hearts of all of us to have more room for the total love that will be heaven.

February 22, 2002

I made a commitment to pray the Mercy Chaplet every day. I am thinking I should also do something merciful for others. To have mercy on slower students? As Von Hildebrand wrote – you can only dispense mercy when you are in control. I could devastate them, but I can choose instead to see them through.

February 24, 2002

Sorrowful Mystery:

Chesterton says that God tells us to love our enemies and our neighbors because generally they are the same persons!

February 27, 2002

We made a trip to the ocean today. I gave You, Jesus, the sorrow that it didn't work to live in the community and teach at the college full time. I tried.

Then I looked at the glorious sunlit ocean. I thought, let me be truly "sonlit" with You, Jesus. Let me be like you, Mary, a hearth of warm understanding for all, not a dragon lady. Jesus promised He would send me the human love I need. Let me trust in that and hope vs. trying to force those to be my friends who I am in conflict with just so I can feel more secure.

Mary says: There is no security on earth. Come, live with us. Now be carefree! Don't worry, be happy.

March 2, 2002

What is Your joy, My Jesus? You say that just as I take joy in my children in spite of their flaws, so You take joy in me.

In the Spiritual Canticle, John of the Cross, #19 wrote, "I no longer tend the herd, nor have I any other word now that my every act is love. If, then, I am no longer seen or found on the common, you will say that I am lost: that, stricken by love, I lost myself, and was found."

Reading this I thought, already now I can begin to let go of the world, just by living most of my week here. The Retreat Center is, in a way, an outer symbol of going out of the world to live in Christ.

March 3, 2002

A long talk with the priest head of the Retreat Center. His theory is that a sensitive child, as I must have been, can take refuge in the mind as an ego defense, not because she is superficial, but because she is afraid of exploding with emotion. Now it is my time of life to recover the sensitive child part as mother to others. To empathize with their sufferings and joys, but not in so close as to explode?

March 4, 2002

Forgiveness in the Our Father prayer presupposes the universal presence of evil, especially in me! By contrast, we can become so eager to refute error that we forget our own sins.

Belloc: "The Church is not something that men fall in love with, but it is home. This was a need. It is the very mold of the mind, the matrix to which corresponds in very outline that outcast and unprotected contour of the soul."

March 5, 2002

Good thoughts from the priest head of the Retreat Center:

Concerning co-dependency: having been made in His image and likeness but as creatures, it was inevitable that we could be tempted to want to be like God ourselves. Part of the Fall is that our God-willed love for each other would be always in danger of being twisted into distorted co-dependency loves. But God uses the neediness to keep us from still worse prideful, independent, or pseudo-god-likeness.

We want to pretend to need no one. Instead He lets us have a foretaste of heaven in the good part of friendship – walking hand in hand. Battling demons alone would be worse. And then He comes to heal and forgive the bad part, bringing good out of evil. I should just take in the pain instead of being bewildered by the bad part and wanting to flee. I should run to you, Mary, and ask for your heart and then be like you, a mother to all, in their miseries. O Mary conceived without sin, pray for us who have recourse to you.

If I put up less resistance, it would help. I could try whenever I get angry to immediately run to you, Mary, and let you expand my heart to allow room for that fierce but sweet compassion. That will be an important part of my spiritual work at the Center.

The Psalm prayer for Tuesday Week 3 says, "Mercy, Lord, our misery is known to us. May no evil desires prevail over us, for your glory and love dwell in our hearts."

There is a hilarious story of the house I am living in on the Retreat Center grounds. The priest head was passing by a street scene where a man was expostulating with a moving company that they were moving his house off the property instead of the house next door they were supposed to haul off. But it turned out that the angry man didn't want the house. Father said he'd take it for the cost of moving, and he plopped it at the Center for a guest house!

I sang the mercy chaplet alone in my guest house. That felt wonderful. Singing to the Father – just myself!

Pere Thomas Philippe, a Dominican priest, wrote in *The Contemplative Life*, "There is a great temptation to lower our ideal so that it will not stand in judgment over us. This is the sin against the light. To sin against the Holy Spirit is to lower one's ideal, to renounce it, to allege that we are not made for that, that there are other things to do, and so forth.

For the first time, I am enjoying being alone – like Kierkegaard's maxim to accept one's self transparently before God?

March 7, 2002

Feeling Jesus bringing me into rapturous prayer, I asked, "Jesus, why so long to bring me back to You in this bridal way?"

I hear You say, "If I had brought you deeper before, you would have quit teaching, and I want you to teach. Now you are in a place where you could finally drop full-time teaching, and I can come to you and make Myself the true center of your heart without losing your work which I need for my Church."

March 9, 2002

Pere Thomas Philippe in *The Way of the Cross* says that, like Veronica, we should venerate the Face of Jesus in the suffering faces of those we encounter. Not to avert the eyes?

Pere Thomas says that Mary has a priestly heart since she is the mother of souls. Does this explain why some widows, in the image of Mary, have a special affinity with seminarians? Like Venerable Conchita of Mexico, who helped found the Missionaries of the Holy Spirit?

Pere Thomas says that after many falls, we should know that Jesus respects our temperament and doesn't simply change it. He wants us to be sweet and kind to ourselves in our falls, and then also to others, even more, the more often they fall. Not to discourage others by having no hope for them because of their faults and sins.

Pere Thomas on the contemplative life: For the contemplative, God alone is enough.

Today is the last day of our long retreat at the Center. I ask you Jesus, what am I afraid of when Your perfect love casts out fear?

That this peace is just a phase? Too good to be true? Something terrible will happen.

What do You say, my Jesus?

"Now curl up into a little ball and let me hold you in My lap and rock you. All of this is to help you live in My heart where it is safe so you don't fear change so much." Amen.

March 15, 2002

I went to confession. The priest said I should go to Therese on giving up gossip and detraction to grow in virtue. Of course, it costs me because I am a lively, amusing person. I should ask for the gift of light humor instead.

I realize that humor is a saving grace all my life, but two-edged, since it means stuffing a lot. (Fleeing from pain into anecdotal humor about the same situations where I felt wounded.)

March 17, 2002

St. John of the Cross: Silence is the speech of God.

March 20, 2002

Pere Thomas Philippe: Complexity comes from trying to be something vs. a simple child.

March 24, 200

At the college, we had a wonderful Christian Passover service. A funny angle was that the head of the order that founded the college has a rule against any alcohol except at planned parties. So, most of us got high very quickly on the Manischewitz wine used in the traditional ceremony.

March 25, 2002

Thinking of some women I know who are immersed in disordered passions, St. Mary Magdalene seemed to tell me that they don't have Jesus as their lover. Pray they may know Him with passion and you, too, Ronda, know Jesus even more. Pant for Him. Eros needs to be transformed, not repressed.

March 27, 2002

Pere Thomas: "The religious habit represents the protection with which the Church envelops us." I read this as applying to my need to have consecrated widows (or later dedicated widows) wearing this simple blue denim garb.

March 28, 2002

Holy Thursday trip to Retreat Center.

Here begins a straight journal of responses to the Holy Triduum rites.

When I came into the small chapel, Jesus threw me immediately into prayer of quiet. I had a feeling of my dear contemplative saints, Magdalene, Teresa, Therese, Edith Stein, and Conchita bringing me here.

Holy Thursday: It seemed as if the head priest was washing the interior souls of the despairing, not just the exterior feet.

Good Friday we had a dramatic procession through the outdoor stations with a priest who has cerebral palsy, staggering down the road carrying a cross.

A poetic sequence I got for the empty tabernacle Good Friday to Holy Saturday evening:

Do You play dead in the tabernacle,

until one of Your lovers comes by,

and You resurrect for us?

Jesus says He is pleased by everything we do for Him in the Church. Like I would be if a grandchild did a picture of me, even if not very good? It is right for me to appreciate it if it is very artistic, but not to get so upset if it is not. As if it were an end, not a means. The end is the I-Thou union.

My daughter, Carla, wrote a poem for Good Friday called,

Purgatory

In the domain of stumblers and stones,
His body waits for me like a cross,
A thing to cling to
When twenty shades of hell
Slant down to cover stalwart faces
Lit by hope.

How many slips and sobs till Paradise?

Here, where sorrowful mysteries circle,
Round for sliding feet,
His tongue cries light,
Flies it with the ravens of this night,
Faint as the shine of feathers
Growing wings.

From a Good Friday poem of Jim Ridley (founder of goodbooksmedia.com and my blog master):

In your dread thurible of parted Flesh

Let now my timid immolation start.

Throw on the gore-sopped wad of rag, my heart;

Or nail it to the beams of that blazing Tree,

Scrap torn from the flag of the enemy.

Burn this sullied ensign of my surrender

Into the banner of Your Victory, Your hidden Splendor.

Pere Thomas Philippe: "Someone with a voluntaristic or willful attitude is able to love, but does not let himself be loved. He closes himself in order to drive ahead. A certain weakness of littleness is wanting to him." This reminded me of a locution I received once when exhausted from being over-extended: "It would be easier for you if you were smaller."

Pere Thomas, again: "The vow of chastity supposes a very great detachment of heart. It allows God to determine the order among our friends. Instead of having personal preferences, we adopt our Lord's choice and are free to love those He asks us to love." "Religious life in community is animated by the charity of hearts that are free."

More of Pere Thomas: "Poverty suppresses the attitude of private ownership that 'incarnates' a person in the world by the extension of himself in his possessions."

"We don't need to get settled in; we don't rent our cell."

Pere Thomas: "God doesn't want His Son to come to earth without being wanted. Mary's longing provided for this."

Jesus to me: "I want you to live in My heart. Here is the deed!" I have freed you from property not so you could settle in at the Center. You are here for a while: our second honeymoon."

More Pere Thomas: "Mary was always in someone else's house in a state of dependence." (St. Joseph, St. John)

I was watching the video *Teresa of Avila*. It was so moving to see her in old age. I ask you, Teresa, what do you want to tell me? You say, "Let Him love you to folly and then you can love Him and everyone else to folly."

JPII, 1994 Pontifical Council of Culture talks of "A voice made peaceful through contemplation of the Eucharistic mystery, like the calm breathing of a soul that knows that it is loved by God."

Mary wants to rescue her brethren from the suicide of sin and so lets her Son plunge her into co-redemptive compassion." Be like her.

April 1, 2002: Easter Monday

St. Francis and I made it to Medicare! A few years before I turned 65, I had no insurance, with Medicare two years or so off in the horizon. Because of my breast cancer years ago, insurance would cost me $1,000 a month. That would be about ½ my income. I prayed and prayed to St. Francis and begged him to make it so that I could use that money to give to the poor (on the basis that Mother Teresa's poor, who are dying, need it now, whereas I just need in on spec) but not have any big health problem before the 2 years were up. It worked!

April 9, 2002

In a spiritual exercise, a late vocation seminarian said that he puts his anger at the foot of the cross and lets Jesus' blood drip on it and then lets the water flow as mercy and peace in proportion to the mercy he needs to show the offender.

April 11, 2002

"Don't hard boil others in their sins," says Julie Loesch Wiley, the pro-life activist. I need to see the wounds of those people I want to judge so harshly.

A priest wrote: "We don't reject the needs and weaknesses of others, their limitations and woundedness, but embrace them, take them upon ourselves and offer the wounds of Jesus for their healing, strength, and redemption."

April 14, 2002

Worried scruple – Do I want to lean on the rich while being poor? Is that really being poor? St. Justin Martyr is quoted in the Office of Readings (p. 540) as saying the rich help the poor, and we are always united. So, I consider that the rich were also enjoined in Scripture to help widows. Widows need security and shelter. That is not wrong.

April 19, 2002

A writer, Lermontov, describing a beautiful mountain scene, "There was peace in heaven and on earth. It was like the heart of a man at morning prayer." Lermontov also says, "We can't help becoming children as we leave social conventions behind and come nearer to nature. All life's experience is shed from us and the soul becomes anew what it once was and will surely be again."

April 21, 2002

A friend I saw when giving a talk in another city told me that all communities have similar problems. I shouldn't try to be a mother, but a grandmother, who has little power.

Jesus says: "Be My merciful love in the world wherever you go. Take all you have learned from life, literature, philosophy, and the saints and turn it into love – I-Thou – Face-to-Face or, rather, let Me turn it into love."

Sense of com-penetration - invisible stigmata?

April 25, 2002

Jesus, how can I get out from under this busyness? "Do less and do it the simplest way, without any false deadlines. Now rest and be carefree 'til you leave vs. finishing everything on the desk. When you get tense about everything, say My Jesus prayer.

April 26-28 – general journal of weekend at the Center:

I come into the chapel alone to say, "It is Jesus. You are waiting for me!" Such an intimate feeling. You say, "Everything that is Mine is yours because you are my bride." Scheming about doing a workshop here at the Center. The Holy Spirit helps me to see that then it would become a place of work. Jesus wants this Retreat Center to be for me as a place of rest, a foretaste of eternity; no pressure. The Holy Spirit seems to say: "You think you are worried about finishing up your work, but really you are afraid not to have the work, as if an abyss of nothingness would open if you really stop!"

Again, Jesus says, "Take it slowly now. Nothing you have on your list has to be done quickly except if you worship efficiency more than Me? Closure? Death is the only closure! Right now, I want you for My saint, to be full of merciful love. Don't postpone that till you finish your work. Pray for those you are in conflict with."

Jesus says, "Poor little red shoes girl. Stop and let me kiss your bloody feet." (The reference is to the film *The Red Shoes*, where the heroine can't stop dancing and finally flings herself down a long stair-case into death. One of her admirers kisses her bleeding feet.)

From a sermon: "There is so much anxiety because we feel so separate vs. the Trinity is One."

April 29, 2002

I am tense about work. Martha, Martha. O Jesus, when will You no longer have to chide me Martha, Martha vs. Mary sitting at Your feet?" "When you trust Me and give up your idols."

April 30, 2002

In a class, we prayed over a young woman with lupus. She said it was one of the most beautiful moments of her life to have us praying over her! (I don't know if it was also physically healing since I left shortly afterwards, but I do so wish, charismatic style, we would always lay hands on people who are suffering.)

May 1, 2002

Today, the workers put up the iron dome of the new Adoration Chapel that is being built for our college. Before classes, a bunch of us stood outside watching the awesome procedure with huge contraptions clasping and lifting the dome. The President was set up with his hard hat to go up in a crane lift and say a special blessing over it. He came down safe and sound and beaming with joy.

A beautiful paragraph from Michael Meaney's manuscript (Dr. Meaney is a philosophy professor and dear friend): "Failing to concentrate on God's love for us tends to reduce our faith to a catechetical acceptance of a set of dogmas about existence, attributes and demands of the Supreme Being, ultimate end or great ideal towards which we ought to direct our lives. However well-motivated this may be, it still radically underestimates Christian life by reducing it to the truest and highest of all ideals. ...Instead of being one ideal among others or even the Great Ideal, Christianity is an Ideal Person. A Godman actively and personally loving us, cooperating with us and incorporating us into the light, life and love of the three Persons of the Trinity. This transcendently true and peaceful experience of profoundly harmonious light, life and love is what we are all hungering for from the innermost recesses of our being."

May 6, 2002

Bernanos, the great French Catholic writer, remarks in a play about Pharisaism: "Pious erudition can keep the Pharisee from ever being surprised by one's own God."

May 10, 2002

After sorting things out, finally sitting down to pray. Jesus, I want to belong somewhere and stay put. You say: "I want to wean you from places so that My heart will be your place. Don't fear. My heart is the best and only safe eternal place. Remember I said in Sedona after you crashed with your own plans, that I want to be able to take you anywhere with me, not alone!"

May 13, 2002

Jesus said that if I slow down, He can show me so much each day, "Each day as you slow down you will be able to see more, blind one!"

May 14, 2002

Sometimes Jesus lets us decide wrongly and then bails us out. He let Joseph think badly of Mary but then changed it around.

May 15, 2002

Two women in Church had some problem with each other. One asked the other in front of us other daily communicants what was wrong. This was before the Mass. It was clear that there were still bad feelings. At the kiss of peace time, one walked way down the aisle and said, "Let's forgive and forget." It was so beautiful to see.

May 16, 2002

From a letter I wrote to the head of a community I left:

"What comes to mind most as I experience so much turmoil in my heart and soul is that being part of any religious community is somehow too complicated for a person like me of such an analytic and justice-seeking bent. I see that others, who are less analytic, and more seeking of pure love without a need to seek justice (a need I believe is God-given to me) are able to offer up the problems with confidence that Our Lady will solve them. I, on the other hand, feel called to be part of the solution...

"In prayer I get a sense that the community is full of holy people, the sacrifices of whom have benefited me greatly. I am deeply grateful, but I would like to take a leave of absence."

May 17, 2002

Glorious Mystery:

Reading Matthew – First, the Lord told Joseph to go to Egypt and then later Nazareth. Messages are indications, not rigid and exact – follow A and at B you'll see C better, is more like it?

May 19, 2002

Email from Russian mission of a community. It is wonderful to see how seemingly useless old people in Russia are taking care of abandoned children.

May 21, 2002

A very loving member of the community left. It feels like trying to swim in an empty pool. How much did he sustain us! We could hardly talk in sentences we were so devastated. I thought- I try to be authentic, but he has heart. Now the heart is gone, and authenticity feels, well, heartless!

Looking at the beautiful ocean, Jesus said, "I want to dazzle you."

May 22, 2002

St. Bernard: Office of Readings. "Where can the weak find a place of firm security and peace except in the wounds of the Savior?"

Office of Readings: "The spiritual man who has been illumined does not limp or leave the path, but bears all things...he is not saddened by the things of time."

A priest suggests asking God to relax each part of you, then breathe in His love and breathe out the pain and resentment. Lines from David Craig's poems based on the Gospel of Matthew: (Check out this wonderful Catholic poet's work. Google it.) "Our sin...starts to fall by degrees, though with Jungian shadows of Death that unclutch our wills so slowly you'd think the darkness charged a fee!"

"He is what lasts, the sun will blink at His look; the stars, no doubt, will lean into Him and learn. But add to this – His power of speech, His deeds! Like he could defeat it all, without bruising a reed."

"In her (Mother Teresa) we saw Jesus's feminine Albanian face, could stable there, in the Wounded Heart she bore. Self-consciousness had no place in her daily rounds. She wanted Jesus to be both fore and ground."

"Hypocrites...they inspect their hands in the morning light, get used to wrinkles...How else will they ever get it right."

"When our houses collapse, we break into a trot."

"And now nothing beyond the God who has us here. And duty? It sounds like jazz to wakening ears."

"Whoever spoke like this? Like the world was His own…He spoke, not about what might occur, but of things that would happen BE-CAUSE He spoke – in the face of lies."

May 24, 2002

En Route to Retreat Center, my new base: Jesus, you seem to say, "Well, we're moving." Just like a husband would say. Jesus telling Nicodemus that he had to be born again. I am thinking that old age is related to this. I should be uttering little helpless cries like a baby. I need to become little, not by thinking but by becoming small and with more heart.

May 28, 2002

I am working on a plan of life for being a Woman of Jesus. Jesus says, "What is most important is that you be with Me every moment of the day: not your prayer schedule! I want to be with you to make you a bride-widow-saint., So just relax, rest in Mary's bosom, so soft and sweet. Mary says she will help with my garb.

(After styling myself as a dedicated widow, or temporarily a Woman of Jesus, I wore different simple blue outfits.)

May 30, 2002

I am editing a novel I wrote about widowhood called *Last Fling*. (It can be found at En Route Books and Media – click on free e-books.)

A book I am reading called *Cold Comfort Farm* has this crude farmer/seducer say that "Women pretend to be interested in a man but all they really want is a man's blood and his heart out of his body and his soul and his pride and after she's got him and he's trapped by his longing for her, she wants to eat him up. He has to defend himself by eating her up instead." Half-truth? Freud asked: what do women want? He thought the answer was that women want a man to control.

Do I like male students because I can control their wildness and they have to obey me?

What do you say, Jesus? "That is what it is like without the God of love. I don't tell My people to pretend evil isn't there; but to overcome it with love."

June 3, 2002

Blessed Angela of Foligno shames me with her love of suffering. I am not she, but I wish to love You in my paltry way. Is that worth something to You? A widow's mite? You seem to say it is good for me to see how far there is to go, but that it is grace, not nature, to love suffering. Rest patiently in My love for now. I want you to love holiness not for fame but for bliss.

June 11, 2002

Gandhi fought for justice with love; not hate, not vengeance. That is what I need to do.

June 15, 2002

Advice for visiting the family: Call on the angels. During their trial the angels had to go from pure intellect to the service of the heart. Pray to the angels of family members to help me see how to help. Conversion goes through sensibility, heart, then intellect. The angels can reach people through dreams, poetic imagination. Angels can bind subtle images. Be sweet grandma and influence them through prayer. Don't try to fix things but just pray to the angels. Don't trust myself. Trying to fix things is workaholism. I need to move through contemplation. I have to pray more and talk less. More spontaneous vs. going through logic. In social situations share anecdotes vs. teaching. Be more playful.

St. Thomas said you cannot know a person through analysis of the mind. You have to love in order to know, because the heart goes deeper.

June 24, 2002: Visit to daughter, Carla, in New Hampshire

You say that You want me to trust. Nothing can happen that You cannot bring out good. I cannot save them, but I can stop talking about it and feel their pain and give it to You. May each one find true love in You and let You expand his/her hearts and souls and minds.

With the family, it is working out well to "bribe" the grand-kiddies into catechism by simply setting up a routine where first we read a chapter, then they get ice cream, and then I play a long game with them of their choice. I bet you, the reader of these journals, would be surprised to see me shooting baskets with them or "lowering myself," to playing simple card games.

Jesus seems to tell me that what matters is not that someone is canonized, but that My love is appeased. Rapture. Eucharist as visible tip of the iceberg of My invisible presence. Compline: "Under his wings you will find refuge." Jesus seemed to say "Turn 'His' to 'Mine' in the Psalms and address it to yourself. "Ronda, under My wings you will find refuge."

June 25, 2002

I was reading about St. Francis, and I decided to make a list of what I really need vs. things I don't need, in order to be more like St. Francis:

Absolutely need: Credit card, food, bedding, spiritual reading, biographies, rosary, paper, Liturgy of the Hours, sack-like purse, phone card, toiletries, pens, checks, teaching materials, addresses of family and friends, copies of the books I wrote, suitcase, clock, coats and 5 winter and summer outfits, watch, glasses, shoes, umbrella, calendar, underwear, manuscripts. I could gradually get rid of the car, the computer, and fiction books.

(Excerpting from these journals in 2019, I have to realize that my hated smart phone eliminates things like clocks and watches, but the computer is even more necessary unless I totally leave the world.)

June 26, 2002

In the novel *The Empty Shrine* by Barrett were these words, "[he] conceives truth to be a liquid which one pours into the jug of his mind. His mind is a good jug, but truth will not take the shape of his container, because it has a form of its own."

Sorrowful Mystery: More anxiety about family problems. Jesus seemed to tell me that "You can't save them, but I can save them."

June 27, 2002

Glorious Mystery: I read a lovely passage in Lloyd Douglas about an Anglican Gothic cathedral – how everything in it forces you to lift your eyes and thoughts upward.

June 28, 2002

A fantastic moment took place in the midst of all the conflicts going on. Peter, Carla's husband, loves gardening. One night, he decided to make a huge fire in the backyard to burn up all the branches lying around. The older grandsons were helping him pile up branches for the fire and whooping it up in the dark of night. Peter wanted a beer, so he yelled to the 2-year-old, who was watching on the porch, to bring him one. The sight of this tot standing at the porch door, naked except for his diaper, grinning and holding out the can of beer, with a huge fire spurting up to the skies was just hilarious.

June 29, 2002

Joyful Mystery: A quiet time with the youngest grandson. They say you can't really understand a child when he/she is with the whole family. You need to be alone with the child.

July 3, 2002

John of the Cross: "Those who seek God and want their own satisfaction and rest...will not find him."

I am old and tired. Holy Spirit, angels, show me what to do better! "Talk less," came the answer immediately. Jesus seemed to add, "Only by letting Me inundate your soul with My love can you stand not to project your personality so strongly."

July 4, 2002

Jesus, make me a peacemaker vs. a time bomb.

I ask El Greco's Christ what does He say about injustice? He says, "I allow it because it weans people away from this world, but I bless those who thirst for justice. It is a seeming paradox. It requires trust – not your greatest virtue! Lack of trust in Me is unjust!"

In the Introduction to the Writings of St. Gertrude, Sister Maximilian Marnau writes: "We have a detailed record of God's dealings with a soul, the personal relationship for which the Creator is willing to stoop with his creature. It is a picture of the Lord as she knew him, including not just his character, his goodness, and his love, but also the manner of his dealings with mankind." God said to Gertrude that He wanted her to write about how He worked in her that others may desire such graces for themselves.

July 5, 2002

Dear Jesus, I am nothing like sweet, sweet Gertrude. How can You love me? You say, "Do I love Teresa less, or Mary Magdalene less? I would like every person I made to be that close to Me. Don't try to be her, but try to be you more in relation to Me!"

"Yes, How?"

"Talk to me about everything. Give me the discomforts, little slights, rancor, moods."

Gertrude speaks of some fit of impatience shown in her words. Jesus says He consumed it in the fire of His love. I need to meditate on how "love covers a multitude of sins."

July 6, 2002

John of the Cross: "The soul that desires nothing but God will not go a long time without a visit." Yes!

To be a saint I would need to entrust every worry and trouble to the heart of Jesus so my burden would be lighter.

This night I got a sense of invisible stigmata. Then it seemed You wanted to know what I would like You to be for me, if I would admit I want You to really be my second bridegroom. Then You said that You cannot delight me because I have put You in a box in my mind.

"You are free, and You should want to free me. First the box was philosophical categories, then you wanted Me to be the same for you as I was for Teresa or Catherine or Gertrude or Edith Stein.

"But, no!" You seemed to say, "I want you to be Ronda of Jesus, someone free and laughing and deep and empathetic at the same time. Hebrew Catholic: Russian, Spanish style. There is so much I can do for you before you leave this earth. Write these journals with great confidence that it is Me and Mine trying to break into your tight little heart."

July 7, 2002

I found my old CD of the *Missa Criolla* and danced to it.

Glorious Mystery: Thinking of last night's locutions, sweet hope of greater happiness. Half sleepy, I lay down on the bed and fell into a sort of floating in grace prayer midway between quiet and rapture. I need to think more about aging and contemplation; about how aging is a gateway to heaven and that we need to overcome the feeling that since we are as ugly as old toads that means God thinks of us that way. Old saints still had contemplative graces of union like Teresa of Avila and John Paul II.

July 8, 2002

I had breakfast this morning with a couple of friends here from the parish. I knew they were going through some heavy trials involving under-employment. The husband quit an excellent job because it had become so impersonal and unsatisfying, thinking he would easily find another one. After a year living on severance pay, it is clear he can't find another good job. He is working for $8 an hour in the meantime selling fish at a supermarket counter. It looks as if they will have to sell their main house and move into a bungalow type house they have in another state just to avoid the mortgage payment.

Since this couple are devout Catholics eager to be saints, I felt it was okay to talk up the joys of simplicity of life. I thought they might take umbrage, but they actually seemed to love hearing about ways to live more simply and austerely, such as making totes and handkerchiefs out of old clothes, washing things by hand, etc. Ideas for less clutter such as saving only the best of what the kids did since first grade vs. all of it, they liked also. I suggested that they ask St. Francis to help them divest. Emanating my own tremendous joy in cutting down for the sake of giving to the poor made it less didactic. Thank you, St. Francis, for inspiring me and letting others be inspired by me even for my so-meager efforts at loving holy poverty.

From a letter from Gabriel Meyer, writer and journalist, relating to some of the current problems:

"The concept of 'happiness' keeps coming to mind. Popular American culture, from Gershwin to the soaps, keys people into the notion that personal happiness is the paramount aim in life to be distinguished from living a useful, productive life. Happiness in the modern sense is focused on the idea that another person can 'save' me, that another person can provide the basis for my own personal fulfillment, that a relationship with an ideal person will solve the problem of my life and place me in a new life condition of happiness and fulfillment. (i.e. through him or her, I will finally get what I really want.)

"But my experience is that happiness does not work that way. First of all, people can't save each other. What they can do, and this is beyond price, is to help each other (the biblical 'helpmate'). How long it takes to realize that friends, not lovers, are the best things in life! And to have the possibility of both in their due and deepening seasons, as committed husbands and wives can..."

(Shades of Tolstoy's Anna Karenina: What she wanted from Vronsky was a kind of passionate salvation, the ultimate lover, and at some point, when the relationship is settled, he turns into another husband, not totally different from the one she fled from to him.)

"Secondly, happiness is not a permanent or stable condition; it is a sense of well-being and beatitude, and, this side of the world to come, it is (in my experience, and by its very nature) partial and elusive (there on Tuesday, overwhelmed by events on Wednesday; glimpsed in a recalled memory or on a stroll; or in the satisfaction of some accomplishment, or in the delight of a beloved; but elusive, a perception, a gift, a 'find,', not a possession, not a state of affairs."

"Paraphrase - in marriage people need the stability of balance – artists need grounded practical people around. Otherwise, if you try to find a similar person, you come up with a brief ecstasy of mutual identity, and then chaos when neither is willing to do the dishes."

July 9, 2002

Joyful Mystery: When my husband and I lived for years with Carla and Peter, they did the cooking marvelously, and I did the clean-up. Then, at various colleges I mostly ate in the cafeteria. In certain ways having cooked for the family some twenty-five years, and not very well at that, I loved any meal prepared by anyone else no matter whether it was gourmet or scraps.

It was only a year ago here in New Hampshire where I have a separate suite with its own kitchen, and at the Retreat Center where I also have my own stove, that I've begun gingerly to plan and cook my own food again. Maybe you know the joke about the man who is ushered into his heavenly quarters by St. Peter. The first evening he looks down to hell and sees a magnificent banquet being served. St. Peter brings him bread and water. This goes on for three days. Finally, our new arrival complains. St. Peter replies: "It's hard to cook for one."

I love to eat but dislike cooking, so I've been buying the simplest things to cook such as chops and steaks and adding stir fry vegetables. This morning I was chopping up the veggies into a pan while a chicken was defrosting in the microwave. It suddenly occurred to me that if I added the chicken pieces to the pan with the tomatoes, eggplant, zucchini, carrots and celery plus some water and bouillon cubes, I would have a sort of chicken cacciatore dish.

This experience probably has to do with a principle my last therapist was eager to get across – take control of your own life! Now, this summer, having decided not to fill every extra moment with writing projects, I have plenty of time for so-called self-nurturing. Offering some of this fare to the grandkids is fun, too. Even if they sometimes sniff at it with disdain since it is not the way Mommy and Daddy used to make it, at other times they gobble it down with relish.

Is it perhaps You, Holy Spirit, who drenches a culture with phrases that may seem far-fetched at first, but really conceal natural wisdom such as "be self-nurturing," or "seek balance," or "brokenness needs healing"? I think so. I find that each of these originally obnoxious-sounding ideas emerges into popularity because there really is some pervasive syndrome out there that people are struggling with poorly. Ultimately, God's love is the answer, but I don't think He minds using human insight as a bridge.

Writing about pop-psychology phrases, there is one that came to mind today: "avoid stuffing pain." I tend to do this. I replace sorrow over something real with worry about something future that might not come to pass.

Today is our wedding anniversary. Martin and I were married in 1962 in an old monastic church in Rome, San Onofrio. Today I am remembering only the beautiful times of our marriage, sensing that his soul is watching over the family left behind. Martin, Martin, wherever you are on the paths of eternity, pray for us. Forgive me for all the ways I disappointed you in life and after your death. You always said I would realize only after your death how much I lost. Well, I do. We will have an eternity to make up for all those feuds. A grace today, perhaps from you, Martin, was to savor all the lovely qualities of our children today rather than worry about their problems.

I received a moving email from my daughter, Diana, in California. She said that nothing I have ever written about the faith or told her impressed her a bit. The only thing that has given her faith in my faith is that I came through cancer, the suicide of my son, her brother; and the death of Martin, my husband and her father. Glory be to you, Father, Son, and Holy Spirit and especially Mother Mary, so close to me in those sufferings. Surely that was sheer grace.

The head priest of the Retreat Center wrote an email saying that if I needed to come back sooner than planned from my summer visit to the family in New England, he would be happy himself to install a better air-conditioner in the guest house I use. I am overwhelmed. It is a long time since any man in authority has considered any physical needs I might have. How generous he is. Praying gratefully about his offer, I thought that it is part of his nature and your grace that he wants to be a refuge for others.

July 10, 2002

I am thinking about Kierkegaard's analysis of resignation and hope. He claimed that hard as it is to resign oneself in detachment from some dearly longed for wish; it is even harder to hope. But without hope we are not ready to welcome the gift of receiving what seemed impossible to obtain. In contemporary psychological terms, resignation, I suppose, involves some degree of control by the self. I may not be able to get what I want, but I can decide how to react assuming I lose. Hope demands a surrender to the person who is beyond our control: God. So even if I get what I longed for, since it was not within my control, I often immediately start thinking suspiciously that something worse. may be just down the road. Better to hope for nothing than hope in a God whose ways are not our ways?

Sorrowful Mystery: My daughter and I had a discussion yesterday about family rights in the case of adults. Do parents and siblings have a right to pressure adult children and sisters or brothers on decisions? Of course, the specific matter is Carla's immediate choices. It is characteristic of Jewish ancestry families, when they are tightly knit, to meddle without scruples in any matter perceived as dangerous to physical or psychological well-being of any member.

After a few hours of talk, I realized that even if I have a right to express deeply believed convictions based on God's truth at least once, and to pray up a storm, I probably don't have any right to apply constant nagging pressure. I surely need to spend some of my time here "letting go and letting God," as the 12-step people put it so well. If I keep commending her soul into your hands, Jesus, I should become less agitated.

Today after the regular morning Mass, here in New Hampshire, while I was sitting quietly in thanksgiving for Holy Communion, a second visiting priest came slowly toward the altar. I would guess his age to be about ninety. Though he was not hunched over, his head drooped low on his chest and his walk was halting. It soon became apparent that he was saying the old Latin Mass but facing the people. I was the only one in the Church but he didn't seem to see me or hear my responses and he didn't ask, as sometimes is done, whether I wanted to receive or not.

Since I was in no hurry, I decided it would be pleasant to stay and place myself in solidarity with all those lovers of the Latin Mass who bewail the infrequency of its celebration. I became a Catholic a few years before the vernacular, so I am familiar with the words of the Latin Tridentine Mass even though I've never studied Latin. The priest said the Mass extremely slowly, whether because of his age or his devotion or both. This gave me ample opportunity to simply gaze at the aesthetics of the thing. There was this grey face surrounded by a circlet of white hair. The oval of his head seemed like a whitish ball that swung the bright red vestments as he turned it from the sacramentary to the chalice back and forth. That white of his hair perfectly matched the white sleeves of the chasuble that protruded from the vestment. Later, the white of the host slowly lifted up in his gnarled hands completed the contrast with the blazing red garment for the martyrs whose lives he was commending. Further contrast was provided by the swaying motion of the vestment and the altar cloth in the breeze coming from a fan some three feet away, and the swift flight of a small bird trying to find its way out of the church.

The Mass took a good three quarters of an hour without any sermon. At the end he intoned the beginning of the Gospel of St. John and then knelt at the foot of the altar for the St. Michael prayer. In a loud voice, I made the responses to these prayers. As he hobbled off holding the covered chalice, I took a chance and very unlike any pre-Vatican II person, yelled out, "Thank you, Father." He turned around and looked at me in the front pew for the first time. With a beatific smile he said, "Thank you for staying. That was the Mass!"

July 11, 2002

Jesus and Mary, I often think of how hot the weather was for long summers in the Holy Land, especially since my visit in May, already unbearably warm for me. There is plenty in the Old Testament about parched earth and thirsting deer, but I don't recall any complaints about it by people in the New Testament. Was that just because parchment was expensive, and so the poor early Christians wrote only about essentials, or was everyone used to it, or were your followers, then, much more ascetical-minded?

I "see" you both smiling indulgently. You seem to want to tell me that you understand those of your children who suffer more than others over physical discomforts. I need not be ashamed or compare myself enviously with those hardier or holier. You urge me to simplify my interior life by humbly confessing my difficulties about all the little crosses of my day. You want me to try to relieve them, and if that is impossible, give them to You and offer them for others in greater spiritual need. Then, don't fret, let go.

July 14, 2002

A friend from more than forty years ago, Stephen Schwarz, came to visit. We are both philosophy professors, so we had a great time discussing ideas. Besides that, I find as I age that there is a type of peace I feel in the presence of old, old, friends that is different from being with newer ones. Continuity, I suppose. He knew me when I was twenty-one and has seen the whole progression from young woman, wife, mother to grandmother-widow? Even though it is almost ten years since my husband's death, it is so strange to have people get to know me who have never known him.

July 15, 2002

Jesus, you once seemed to tell me to not be so New Yorker-ish in being suspicious of blue-collar people. Here is a confirmation. I went to the local mechanic to see about my flat tire. They were such a happy band of workers – three men joking with each other throughout in their small shop. Even though it was obvious I was clueless and they could have sold me a brand-new tire, they checked out the flat one, sealed it, and said to come back to test the air tomorrow morning. If I needed more help, then I could pay them $8 for the job!

I praised them lavishly and promised I'd tell all my friends to go to them. Perhaps wearing a large crucifix has something to do with it. Sometimes a Christian, whether Catholic or not, seems to be helpful because of You. Some of them say something like, "what a pretty cross you're wearing." Even though such a comment is kind of spiritually gauche in the sense that my battered old crucifix is hardly pretty or meant to be, I realize the sentiment behind it is, "I love Him, too."

Last night, I was reading Caitlin Thomas' book about Dylan Thomas' death and her widowhood. Here is a fascinating account of her sentiments now that she is alone. Before, she used to complain greatly about her housewifely rounds, but now: "Then I could wholeheartedly revile my fate, and say I was meant for better things. But now I have got better things, and only myself to revile, what do I do but complain about my lack of chains, and go searching, and screeching, and banging into walls, like a blinded demented hen, looking for a master to tell me what to do, and when; so that, presumably, I shall have the pleasure of doing the opposite again. For that is another of those little bittersweet ironies, that wrongdoing loses its savor when it is made permissible; and only the unprocurable is a luxury. So now that nobody cared what I did, nor tried to stop my exaggerated exhibitions of myself, just to show I was afraid of nothing, the bite was deftly taken out of the apple. And replaced by a quaking aspen leaf, that was me, not sure of which foot to put in front of the other, in which direction to turn my eyes, stumbling, belatedly newly born, wandering, bereft, in a dense country of confused woods, stifled by too many trees."

Today is the feast of St. Bonaventure. In the Office of Readings was one of my favorite selections from his book *The Journey of the Mind to God.*

"Seek the answer in God's grace, not in doctrine; in the longing of will, not in the understanding; in the sighs of prayer, not in research; seek the bridegroom not the teacher; God and not man; darkness not daylight; and look not to the light but rather to the raging fire that carries the soul to God with intense fervor and glowing love. The fire is God, and the furnace is in Jerusalem, fired by Christ in the ardor of his loving passion...

Let us die, then, and enter into the darkness, silencing our anxieties, our passions and all the fantasies of our imagination. Let us pass over with the crucified Christ from this world to the Father. Surely this was not written to cause us to neglect doctrine, understanding, teaching and light, but to long for the goal of truth, union with the persons of the Trinity. Philosophy is the handmaid, not the Bridegroom. When, finally, will I embrace you, my God, with all my heart, rather than clinging to the idea of you, instead, with my mind?

Writing about holy persons, John of the Cross says that "they ordinarily bear in themselves an 'I-don't-know-what' of greatness and dignity. This causes awe and respect in others because of the supernatural effect diffused in such persons from their close and familiar conversation with God."

What a good description of the founder of the order that runs the college. In his presence I usually feel as if wafted into an ante-room of heaven.

July 16, 2002

A friend of mine is searching for a good school for a son of hers in the state they are moving to. The anguish in finding that the public schools are likely to be full of delinquent kids and the Catholic schools are probably led by those with dissenting opinions is a serious problem. Because of his learning disabilities, she doesn't feel equipped to homeschool him. Listening to my friend's worries woke me up once more to how important it is to be teaching in or founding new Catholic schools loyal to the magisterium. Please, Holy Spirit, speed on these initiatives and give courage to those already ministering in this way to deal with the practical problems of such projects.

Today is the feast of Our Lady of Mt. Carmel. One of the readings from mid-afternoon prayer included these lines: "The gentle will inherit the earth. They will have peace to their heart's content." Relating these words to being a bride of Christ as a dedicated widow, I thought: The bridegroom wants to bring the bride to a state of detached peace. He doesn't do this by forcing her to control her errant emotions. Instead, it is the sweetness of the grace He pours into her soul that leads her to surrender, and then as a result, she is less concerned about lower things.

I thought that we cannot give up the craving for happiness on this earth except through foretastes of heaven becoming so beautiful that we can let go of our worldly hopes. John of the Cross doesn't mean that holy people have no emotions, as the Stoics tried to attain, but that these feelings are purified of wildness and excess.

July 18, 2002

In John of the Cross' *The Spiritual Canticle,* he writes that in the spiritual marriage the soul becomes divine through participation insofar as is possible in this life. I find it clarifying to my students when they hear of New Age gurus who claim that the soul is divine. Often, they make it seem as if there is no transcendent God – only the divine within the human soul or the world. Sometimes, then, they take sentences out of context from Jewish and Christian writers to show that all religions believe in the divinity of the soul.

The key word is "participation." To partake of something is not to be identical to it. The light of day participates in the sun. It isn't the whole sun. In eternity the blessed will be in the closest possible union with the divine, but each one will not become a god or goddess.

John of the Cross also writes that to the bride, he (Christ) communicates His ways of redemption with remarkable ease and frequency. Perhaps this is one more citation I can use to show that locutions are not necessarily illusory, even for those less advanced in the spiritual life.

I keep wondering if I am belaboring this point out of fear of ridicule or simply sensitivity to some reader's natural doubt. It helps me, Jesus of the Sacred Heart, to consider that You literally died to win our hearts in repentant gratitude. Some doubters of locutions seem to think of You as sitting like a spectator on top of a mountain laughing at us, Your children, as we keep falling back down the hill. I want to see You, instead, as hovering over us with loving-kindness, eager to encourage us in whatever way we will accept, whether it be locutions, visions, or the many personalized gifts of daily life such as a favorite hymn sung at the moment someone needs it most. I find that Catholics with less of a love for words and more for sensation, will find God encouraging them through natural beauty.

July 19, 2002

Perhaps because sitting on the floor to pray is hard on the body, I have begun slowly to add some sacred dance to my time at Your feet, Lord. I play the *Missa Criolla* – marvelous Argentinian music composed in the 60's to which my sister choreographed a passionate and inspiring dance many years ago. Even though I am a clumsy ox, it does my soul good to have the body take the lead in prayer, at least occasionally.

Also, I absolutely need exercise but can't stand making myself a moving prey to the mosquitoes as happens always on summer walks. When this part of my family moved to a forest area in New Hampshire, I had such happy visions of these strolls. No more. In spite of repellant and post-bite fluids, these are big annoying bites that last a week. So, dancing about my room is good for me.

The Jewish people rock back and forth when they pray. Some charismatic Christians dance in the spirit. I wonder if you danced when you were alone, Mother Mary? And You, Jesus? I have a sense You are telling me there were ritual religious dances and ways women danced on special occasions, too.

Sorrowful Mysteries: When I first came this summer, I had *Lives of the Saints* to read before closing my eyes at night. Now that I have run out of these, I am selecting books off the old family shelf, hoping to learn something as well as turn my mind away from heavy problems besetting me at this time. One of these books I was dipping into was upsetting since it forced me to face dreadful realities on the social scene I try not to think about too much. It was a book written in 1925 called *The New Negro*. It contains articles, poetry, fiction, and drama coming out of what was called the Harlem Renaissance. Since my mother was one of those New York City white people with many black friends of those arty circles, I have always had an interest in this period of black urban history between the two World Wars.

What made it sorrowful to read was the projection in the optimistic articles of a seemingly certain progress toward equality and appreciation between blacks and whites. The violent horrors of black liberation with the continuance even after partial victory, of racism, discrimination, family dissolution, crime, drug-addiction and abortion, was not foreseen even by those whose writings displayed the seeds of these destructive forces. The black ministers preaching hell-fire for the sins of their people were depicted for the most part as comic or tragic figures, but not as prophets of still worse immorality. Black saints, intercede for your people. Help them come back to their Christian roots. Let the non-violent mission of Martin Luther King, Jr. and his followers remain to inspire the people to the values that can save them from bitter despair. (Later I was glad to discover that Alvita King, Martin Luther King, Jr.'s niece, is a tremendous pro-life speaker, especially informing others of the black genocide agenda of many pro-choice institutions.)

I also read a novel by Tom Clancy called *Without Remorse.* I rarely read thrillers but since this writer is so popular, I decided I could do with more of a slice of the culture I don't belong to. This helps me in teaching since many of my students are much more immersed in that culture than I am. If I illustrate a point in philosophy with examples from a best-seller, especially if it was made into a movie, they get the point instantly.

The plot involved a good-guy Navy Seal who, on returning from duty in Vietnam, gets mixed up in fighting a drug ring that includes young prostitutes who are tortured and killed in the line of duty by their pimps. We gradually watch our sensitive, strong, noble Navy man develop into a kind of terrorist, taking the law into his own violent hands. At first it looks as if the moral of the novel is that terrorism is wrong even against bad guys. Instead we are worked into thinking that individual vendetta is justified. While it could be that we have reached a point of moral chaos in our country such that the author's point is worthy of serious debate, the depressing part was how the violence was depicted with a kind of gleeful abandon. Since he is a best-selling writer, there must be many who enjoy such scenes.

Father God, you proclaim that vengeance is Yours, and that even in legitimate self-protection or national defense we need to flee from hatred. How far from this are we? As the philosophers of peace from Tolstoy to Gandhi to Martin Luther King, Jr. are eager to show, there can be no peace in society if our hearts are full of violence – inner hate, verbal hate displays, or physical force. So, let peace begin with me by always giving me Your love so that the feeling and the word "hate" will never be part of my soul and language.

The hymn reads: "You (God) are the spirit's tranquil home. In you alone is hope fulfilled." The part that moved my heart was "in you alone is hope fulfilled." Amen. No more hoping foolishly in perfect people, perfect colleges, perfect communities. We need to try always to advance the good, but our hope must be in You alone.

July 20, 2002

This week, thousands of young people will go to World Youth Day in Toronto. I have seen kids with little faith, pushed to attend by their parents, come back blazing apostles. Lord, break through the defenses, heal the wounds, and send them forth into this sad world of ours.

July 30, 2002

I was invited to a Carmelite monastery. There was a large wooden statue of Little Therese. A little above ground level, she was elevated in such a way that it was possible to take one of her open hands and to hug her habited form. Even though the sculptured face was not your actual face, it seemed as if you were truly present for me there, my beloved St. Therese.

Behind the nuns there was a painting made by their superior of Jesus, good shepherd, holding a lamb in His arms. What was unusual was the way it almost seemed as if You, Jesus, was making eye-contact with the lamb. The sense of You being a lamb of God and my being Your lamb was poignant.

One of the Sisters said that we could only be happy if we were making God happy. An evocative statement! Yes, dear Jesus, let me get it that simple. It is like St. Thomas saying you can only love yourself loving.

July 31, 2002

I was overwhelmed by the canonization of Juan Diego, seen on EWTN. What a sense of your universal Church, Our Lady of Guadalupe. You know you are my favorite apparition – I think because of the incredible beauty of your Mexican face and your being a pregnant mother. When the Aztecs came out dancing during the ceremony, I called my sister, the sacred dancer. With an unexpected deep sob from the gut, I said "One day we will be in heaven with no more tears and conflicts. We will sing and dance together in heaven."

Jesus says when you are scared, you have to hold on tighter to Me. Yes! Yes! Yes!

Since I was packing up the Office of Reading book for my return to the college, I read ahead from the writings of the saints for all the days until August 16th.

Some quotations:

St. John Vianney said: "This union of God with a tiny creature is a lovely thing. It is a happiness beyond understanding. My little children, your hearts are small, but prayer stretches them and makes them capable of loving God."

Another reading mentions that St. Dominic was cheerful. St. Clare says that the fragrance of Jesus revives us from the dead!

August 2, 2002

In Ephesians 4:29-32 Paul says "Say only the good things men need to hear."

August 6, 2002: Feast of the Transfiguration.

I especially love this feast day. I always remember a comic but actually wonderful moment Martin and I had at the actual Mount of Transfiguration in Israel. My husband hated charismatic renewal. When he occasionally went to some conference, he alone among thousands crossed his hands over his chest while all the others, including me, of course, were waving our arms in the air in praise. It happened that a pilgrim bus arrived at the Mount just as we were about to enter the Church. The pilgrims lifted their arms in praise as they came off the bus. Suddenly Martin raised his arms, too. I snapped a photo, thinking he was doing it in jest, and it would be fun to have the photo some days/years from then. Seeing the photo years after, Martin remarked that he hadn't been mocking charismatics. He actually felt a great grace to praise God in that way at that moment!

(Author's Note: I WROTE MANY OTHER JOURNALS AFTER THIS TIME SPANNING YEARS IN NORTH CAROLINA WITH MY FAMILY AND AT HOLY APOSTLES IN CONNECTICUT. IF YOU FIND THE ENTRIES YOU JUST READ TO BE HELPFUL, YOU CAN FIND MORE OF THESE BY GOOGLING *6 TOES IN ETERNITY* – FOR FREE ON THE WEBSITE OF EN ROUTE BOOKS AND MEDIA.)

"God Alone Is Enough"

"Seek ye first the kingdom of heaven and its righteousness and all things will be added unto you." Matthew 6:33

In 2008, I was living in an apartment near Carla's family in North Carolina. At exactly 3 AM in the morning, I woke up suddenly. It seemed as if the Holy Spirit wanted to teach me certain truths. I wrote them down. This continued every night at 3 AM for 3 months.

These were not messages of prophecy to the world in any sense. However, because they seemed so full of truth that could benefit many readers, with the help of my dear friend, Dale Noble, I later assembled them into a booklet entitled: *God Alone!* Hindsight, I thought that since they came shortly before I left for a long teaching period of seminarians, Sisters, and lay students at Holy Apostles College and Seminary, the "messages" were to form me into a better person.

I love these "messages," but if you don't, just skip ahead to the next chapter about my life as a retired great-grandmother.

Note: In the messages, the Holy Spirit used the plural "We" for the "voice" of the teacher. Other times it seemed clearly to be the "voice" of someone else, such as St. Paul. When the "voice" said "we," I interpreted that as being the "we" of the Trinity. But I prefer to just leave it as "We" because "The Trinity" sounds presumptuous if it turns out it all came out my own "unconscious." I think they came from God simply because they are not what I would usually teach myself, but seem to come from a higher perspective.

May 13, 2008

To prepare for eternity, We want you to appreciate the beauty of creation and life even more, but also to relax your grip on it. Let yourself be wafted a little bit above everything, as if you were levitating.

About the Moral Law: "Straight is the gate and narrow the way...." (Matthew 7:14)

St. Paul: Sin seems like liberation but turns to dust. You experienced this. In these times on the globe there is a clearer understanding of this because of the publicly viewed excesses and catastrophic penalties in the flesh. The hope of joy in procreative marital sex has been veiled because of divorce where the children can become pawns. So, the young people don't feel the secure nest. There is need for strong open witness about the brambles on the strayed path and the goodness of the straight path. This is being done in some contemporary Christian teaching on chastity, where the witnesses are open about their experience. You need freedom in the Spirit to be honest... for the sake of liberation from a society as crazed on this as the pagan societies I preached to. To be chaste, people have to cleave to Jesus as I did with passionate constant prayer.

May 14, 2008
More about the Moral Law

Holy Spirit: We need the moral law because humans are so greedy about trying for heaven on earth in following their illusions that worldly goods will make them happy, such as stolen possessions or the pride of fame. Just the same, it is not as if once someone sins, We give up on them and totally reject them. No. We let them live in the consequences of their wrong choices. The "righteous" want to see a clearer punishment, such as the immediate destruction of the body of the sinner. This is because the "righteous" are tempted and jealous of the seeming good the sinner got by breaking the code. The "righteous" then feel frightened that the other sinners "got away with it." In this way, concupiscence (greed for bodily satisfactions such as lust, gluttony, possessions) and pride make a vicious circle.

Both the concupiscent and the proud are motivated by fear: fear of not having enough, which leads to covetousness. The fear of being a wretched coveter instead of a proud Stoic (self-sufficient person) leads to sins of anger and desire for vengeance, and trying to be victorious through denunciation. Do you see how Jesus tried to unmask these double evils by condemning greed and lust but also condemning self-righteousness? What is the way out of the circle? "Perfect love casts out fear." (1 John 4:18) By offering you the perfect love of the Trinity and, through the centuries, the comfort of the love of your spiritual mother, Mary, and the model of so many saints and Holy Communion (communion with us), we try to reach into you to open the knots of fear.

As Our love finds a place in you, We build a well in the depth of you in which to gradually pour in grace which over time overflows so you can love your neighbor as yourself. You see? When your well of love is fuller, you can love yourself and reach out to your neighbor with loving concern as you see them grabbing out of fear and judging out of fear. It takes a long time to work out. The process is called "life." It is Our "job" and Our joy to see how to overcome the obstacles in you that come from original sin, childhood wounds, social formation, and your "frightful" choices. "But, be of good cheer for I have overcome the world." (John 16:33)

May 15, 2008
The Family

Holy Spirit: Out of individualism, you think too much as if each individual has to have every virtue to be complete, whole and perfect. Your critical eye focuses on each one in a family and you think about each one's defects, and your mind works on how you would like each one to be. The same with your family in the Church. You have not really understood the mystical body image We gave you in Scripture. (Jesus is the head; you are the body or the idea that a hand is not a leg.) It would be better if you look at each one and be grateful for every virtue, talent and good personal way each one has, and see how it contributes to the family and other places this person is: school, work, Church. They need the help of the Spirit to perfect those qualities to bring them under the umbrella of love. In their areas of defect, when some capacity is needed by the Spirit, they need to call for help on those who are better in this area and to seek Divine help. But they don't need to berate themselves constantly for not being everything. That comes from a proud, competitive, envious, spirit.

This teaching is part of the goal We have for greater appreciation for your own gifts and the gifts of others. It will take away tense striving and make "the burden light." You will be without so much tension to be perfect in a worldly way. The fierce desire to control others and yourself must give way to giving yourself and others to Us in prayer and becoming encouragers and affirmers of the good.

May 16, 2008

(I woke suddenly with images of war. I have been reading about the Vietnam War and the Iraq war).

Jesus: Wars are a shock treatment (We permit) to break through the dreadful complacency of worldliness. What is important is not your analysis, but the cracking of the shell – the breaking through the illusion that you and others can make a paradise out of combined selfishness. In the soul open to the need for God's love and for salvation, those instincts (for survival) are transformed in solidarity with others as you see in magnified form in the saints who didn't choose evil as a desperate means for survival.

May 17, 2008
Healing

Jesus: In healing, try to see what the demon is of that problem. When I was on earth, I often cast out demons. I didn't act as if "demons" was only a symbolic name for vague human forces. So, in asking for healing for yourself and for others of sin, it is helpful to ask to be delivered from that demon, say, of drugs or anger. It keeps you from belittling the problem or from acting as if these problems are just natural and inevitable reactions to exterior events in your lives.

About Conversation

Holy Spirit: There is a roughness in your talk, not only as in talk among embattled soldiers full of vulgarity and cursing, but also within your families. Teasing can be a form of fondness, but I am advising you to avoid harshness or the indifference of not greeting each other with words or gestures or smiles of welcome. It leads people to become shut up in cold defensiveness and then to seek relief sometimes in the camaraderie of shared addictions or in solitary addictions where there is a note of tenderness toward the self: such as "poor me. This drink will make me feel better, or this masturbation, this over-indulgence in food makes me feel good."

(Author's Note: I did not interpret the Holy Spirit to mean ordinary pleasures in life, but addictions.)

Politeness is good when it is an expression of respect, but it is even better when it overflows from solidarity and goodness of heart towards others in daily life. Watch the way genuinely loving people conduct themselves in these small aspects of life such as light humor, affection, affirmation. Don't write this off as convention but learn from it and plunge yourself into the source: God the Father, "from whom comes all good gifts." (James 1:17)

May 18, 2008
Hospitality

Holy Spirit: Your homes, your doors, your arms, should be open wherever possible. How sad. So many locked houses and locked up personalities, as you say. Yes, sometimes, locks are necessary. We know that, but it should be a sadness for you that this is so. The house of Jesus, Mary, and Joseph was always open. The heart of Mary was wide open to the incarnation in her constant prayer; she let God stretch her – now you are rightly calling her the spiritual mother of the world.

Are some of you even self-protected against God your Father, your Creator? Like Adam and Eve after the Fall, do you hide from God rather than walk with Him? We miss you. A mother of a large family always knows when one does not come to the dinner table. We miss you when you don't come to the Eucharistic table. Unless you respond to the call with an open heart, how can you receive the Eucharist?

You have a thousand reasons to be locked in on yourself. We understand. But We knock. This time, open the door.

May 19, 2008

Holy Spirit: ...your culture is dominated by statistics and cynicism. This (the teachings of Jesus) is not a PR campaign. It is to be a transition for hearts. Have you not been changed? Was it so easy for you to become more loving (by will power alone) that you want to doubt that the Source is directly working on your transition? "Love is patient, love is kind" ... you are all too inclined to impatient harshness...You are in training.

May 22, 2008
Our Church

Holy Spirit: Those working to heal divisions in the Church sometimes want to minimize the splits so they can have hope. We want, through love, to open each side to the truths which will enable each of you to let go of attachments to errors and half-truths. The truths that set you free are known to you already, but are veiled, not only by false philosophies, but also by lack of deep spirituality. Notice that in the midst of all the ecumenical and interfaith dialogues, John

Paul II called leaders together in Assisi for a retreat. If you are called to help heal divisions, you must become closer to those around you. Before, you would feel too angry with them to want to get to know them better.

(Author's Note: a reader wondered if this locution could be seeming to say the errors that divide don't matter. I replied that I thought it meant that experts should work on those thorny issues in ecumenical dialogue but that some of us, I included, would be better off trying simple love and prayer.)

May 23, 2008
The World Around You

Holy Spirit: Begin to link your own heart to all the pain and joy in the world in a cosmic yet personal sense. We don't want our children to be insular or global but deep and at the core and in touch with the hearts of others suffering and joyful. You tend either to groveling despair or grandiose pride. But Jesus is high and lifted up on the cross with the seed of resurrection real but hidden. When you cleave to Jesus, Mary, and Joseph in prayer, you are mystically in touch with everything at the core. You are not narrowly chained to the local or national, but this is not for the sake of making theories about the past, present, and future, but to be able to love everyone through loving each individual who appears in your life. By talking to you in this way, We want to unite your head and heart and will, imagination, and spirit.

We can simultaneously stretch and deepen you when you truly surrender in trust. Fear constricts, and pride of ambition gives a false transcendence. Trustingly walk slowly, taking in, responding and then, as Jesus proclaimed, all will be one as I and the Father are one.

May 24, 2008
Poverty of Spirit in Battle

Holy Spirit: When you are in a battle for the cause of truth, for Christendom; or to witness to your own personal values, you have an arsenal of words, your favorite weapons, that worked when others tried to convince you; they give you symbolic victory, words of Ours to bolster your truth with authority, sometimes taken out of context. I am the Spirit of Truth. When in conflict, I want you to come to Me with the openness of the poor in spirit. This is not because there is no truth... There is personal truth as well as present day application. But, to let the truth shine through you, you have to be less defensive and really seek Me to give you the words that pierce, not like a dagger of hate, but like a two-edged sword of LIGHT.

May 27, 2008
Light and Darkness

Holy Spirit: When you become more silent, you can see in yourself and in others the twisted rays of light and dark in ways of life and character. You feel frightened, as you would say, alienated, from others and from yourself. When you feel alienated from others, you want to hide in yourself, but then when you feel alienated from yourself, where do you go? You have to run past any limiting images of Us, to the real God the Father, Son, and Holy Spirit, and Mary, to our real presences so that you can hide in Us and become more like Us to get light and love for others with less darkness and fear (defensiveness).

This process of transforming you doesn't take place in a way that is clear to you. That is why trust is so important. Often what you consider darkness is shadow, and what you run to as light is glitter. But We don't sit on high laughing at your struggles. We are cheering you on for each tiny victory when you see goodness where previously you were too defensive to notice, or where someone you think is critical and unappreciative ratifies what you are doing. The closer you come to Us, the Light, the greater will be your yearning, so that others and you, yourself, can be only light.

May 28, 2008
Together

Holy Spirit: Much of the time my children are knotted up in power struggles because of fear and pride. That makes it hard for you to benefit from all the ways you can help each other. In your generation, where so many live very long, but in a weakened condition, you are forced into greater inter-dependence. This rankles, but gradually opens you to greater detachment from this earth and eagerness for total dependence on heaven. The Church is a school of good inter-dependence because you need the self-donation of the priest for your daily heavenly bread in the Eucharist, and he cannot fulfill his ministry without your coming to receive, and all your works of love.

But, why is it so hard, you ask? For those of you who work in the parish, the more you want it to be heaven on earth, the harder it goes. It can be the healing of your individual family wounds as you grow in love, but it can never satisfy you the way full union with Us, the Trinity, the angels and saints, will be in heaven. We want you to cultivate gratitude for the tiniest gifts you receive each day from others in every part of your life. Yes, even for the charm and comfort of your pets. And then to let Us, in the Sacraments and prayer, fill you with Our love. This way you can be healed of all that pride and fear that pushes you to over-react to every annoyance, and set-back. To come into this good way of being together in preparation for heaven doesn't require a plan. It is rather a yielding to impulses throughout the day and the leadings of your angel.

"The fruits of the Spirit are love, patience, joy..."

May 30, 2008
Breaking Down Barriers

Holy Spirit: In the Trinity and in Paradise, there were no barriers. Satan created the first barrier in his revolt, and then Adam and Eve set up a barrier by disobeying God. They exiled themselves from Us in this way. The physical exile was an outward barrier, the closed gates guarded by angels. Jesus' "all will be one" prophecy and vision removes the exile. "The veil of the Temple cracks" at the moment of His crucified death.

You as humans experience this pattern in microcosm. You begin a friendship with joy, feeling kinship and openness. Then come the surprising negatives, and you exile yourself from each other. Instead you are to run to the heart of Jesus, dragging your image of your friend with you, and beg for healing love. Beg that the love of God in both your hearts can leap over the barriers or break them down. Simply, you could pray: O God, I delighted so much in the light and goodness I saw in my friend. Now he or she seems like a knot of anger and fear with no room for me. I feel pushed out. I don't know how to be with this person.

And perhaps you could hear Us say something like: Keep lifting him or her into our light, and trust that either now, soon, or in eternity, the love you had for one another will be purified and free of all barriers. Then forgive whatever part the other one has in that barrier, and ask forgiveness if you are at fault, also. Then ask simply: Today is there anything I can do to show love and understanding to my friend? A prayer, a word of empathy if nothing else? And when you see your friend, ask Us for a clue about what is still possible between you. Love is a gift from Us, not a bargain the other failed to fulfill, where you got damaged goods for a high price! In a way it is like that, but you were also damaged goods. (As the poet Auden wrote) "Thou shalt love thy crooked neighbor with thy crooked heart."

May 31, 2008
Retirement

Holy Spirit: You think of this with emotions that waver between relief and doubt. We think of it as a big time of preparing you for your eternity. For many of you, it is a time of increased physical pain and woes. These We use as purifications and ways to detach you from the earth and ready you for your voyage to your true home. It shortens the time of purgatory which is a purging of the vileness that narrowed your hearts. You need so much more space for graced love for your hearts to be ready for heaven.

It is a wonderful time for witnessing to those younger than you. By your joyful eagerness to be united to Us in heaven, they get to see the deeper meaning of life, beyond survival and coping. Of course, they cannot see this if they think of Our faces as filled with judgment of them. When you cannot avoid seeing their sins and faults, let that look from you be more sad, rather than angry. "Dominus flevit." (The Lord wept looking over Jerusalem) (Luke 19:41)

Think often of the older days in the lives of our saints. (Ronda: I thought of Teresa of Avila dying with her head on the lap of her favorite Sister-friend. I thought of old Cardinal Newman doggedly persisting, hearing confessions for hours in cold confessionals, of Mother Teresa on her death bed telling us to be grateful for the beautiful things in life such as being able to walk. I thought of John Paul II when asked why he still showed himself to audiences when he was in such terrible condition, saying: "They must see how I suffer for them.")

June 2, 2008
Family

Holy Spirit: You would like it to be all the good part: the long under-

93

standings from proximity through the generations; the physical closeness; the built-up gratitude for all the helps. We understand that, after all, we created the family. But, then, there are the swift judgments born of long knowledge; the resistance to compromise as each digs in with prideful self-defense; the love dished out in spoonfuls that more be not demanded. And from this you flee back to friendship love, lighter, less painful but less primordial, less of the gut.

We understand, We created friendship. You hope your own marriage and children would have all the best of family and friendship; in the image and likeness of what was best in your past families, but free from all the tangled grief and disappointments. We don't dash your hope. We wanted, by Our grace, to transform everything natural through supernatural virtues and gifts into its best form.

Each time anyone in the family opens to grace, there is more love, more joy, more peace. Each time one in the family closes the heart to the others and to Us, there is less love, joy and peace. We urge you into the arms of forgiveness, to heal the rifts, and to make new beginnings. Even when on earth the bonds break, We aim for final restoration in our home, which is called heaven.

June 3, 2008
Closeness

Holy Spirit: You are ambivalent about closeness. Sometimes two of you can work together, your gifts complementing each other, but very often to try to do things together is to clash; each one slowed down by the resistance of the other, such as trying to put the collar on the cat's head while she is trying to keep it off.

You transfer this ambivalence to your relationship to Us. You think if you get closer to the Father, He will try to make you do what doesn't fit your personality, as your human fathers sometimes did. You think if you get closer to God the Son, you will be crucified; you think if you let Me guide you moment by moment, My fire will burn up all your own precious goals.

Try to think of it more like a cello and a violin in a duet. Yes, there is a score, but the violin has a different part than the cello. It is not drowned out by the cello, and there comes about a beautiful harmony when each one does its own part well; much more beautiful than if the violin player just plays his or her own melody unrelated in any way to the will of the composer.

To avoid frightening you, We don't tell you moment by moment what Our part is in your thoughts, words and deeds. We want you to learn the main pieces We can play together "by ear." We want you to hear when you are playing off key, reacting instead of responding, lashing out rather than forgiving...Yet We have no trouble with the harsh notes, We can gather them up into a high harmony if you let Us. To see if you are playing with Us, listen. When you are playing with Us the sound is called love. "The greatest of these is love." (1 Corinthians 13:13)

June 4, 2008
Means and Ends

Holy Spirit: You become insecure often because you make means into ends. These messages are a means, not an end. Think of St. Faustina, told that the new order would be founded before she died. (It wasn't physically founded but it was spiritually founded and then started after her death.) We propose a means and if you accept, We move with that, but if there is too big an obstacle, then We try another means. Other possibilities are other means for furthering the end, which is union with Us. So, you must become closer to Us right now and not cling to specific means.

The messages are good means, but they might not go on the rest of your life. Jesus wasn't on earth until the end of time! We understand that you cling to a means because you experience closeness to Us through it or you think you will get closer through it. That is fine, but We don't want you to be frightened if there is a change.

(Ronda: But the sacraments and the Church aren't just changeable means, are they?)

Holy Spirit: No, they are Us. However, we also work through other paths as John Paul II explained in *Threshold of Hope,* with the Catholic Church being the direct beam of light to the world but other rays off it participating in that light.

June 5, 2008
Spiritual Warfare

Holy Spirit: You cannot help wishing for rest from the combat, and you are startled to have to go back to the battlefield when you thought that victory was won. Only in heaven will that battle be over. On earth, how can you win at all if your guard is down? If you don't call for reinforcements? That doesn't mean that you need to be tense. More that you must be aware. The sign that the enemy is near is that sense of disequilibrium; unexpected hostile winds; change of moods in those usually friendly. But your weapon is not the sword, or the shield; but sacraments and prayer; unexpected love piercing through another's defenses as We pierce through yours. All these weapons we give you for free, for We are an army of liberation from your fear and theirs. "You know not the day nor the hour." (Revelation: 3:3)

(Before adding messages for the second set, I have been impressed by how often in Scripture and in the prayers of the Liturgy of the Hours there are references to being guided in life by God. Before receiving this steady stream of locutions, I would have been inclined to think that these words about being guided meant the guidance already given in Revelation in scripture and tradition, but now I am thinking they could also be alerting us to the possibility of the kinds of "words in the heart" I have been receiving.) You, the reader, might want to pray something like: "Holy Spirit, I am reading these messages Ronda thinks are from You. If it would help to make me more holy, that is, more full of love of God and neighbor, to receive closer guidance through messages, please open me to receiving them.")

Here are the passages I found that seem to point to the possibility that the "messages" are from God.

From the Psalms:

"Bring me to your holy mountain, to the place where you dwell."

Psalm Prayer, Tuesday, Morning Prayer, Week II: Almighty Father, source of everlasting light, send forth your truth into our hearts and pour over us the brightness of your light."

Psalm 49: "My lips will speak words of wisdom; my heart is full of insight. I will turn my mind to a parable..."

Psalm Prayer for Psalm 49 Tuesday Evening Prayer Week II: Make our mouths speak your wisdom, Lord Jesus..."

Psalm 86: Turn your ear, O Lord, and give answer for I am poor and needy...Show me, Lord, your way so that I may walk in your truth."

Psalm Prayer for Psalm 142 Sunday Evening Prayer II, Week 4:

"Lord God, you are the eternal light which illumines the hearts of good people."

Isaiah 2:2-5..." Come let us climb the Lord's mountain, to the house of the God of Jacob, that he may instruct us in his ways and we may walk in his paths. For from Zion shall go forth instruction and the word of the Lord from Jerusalem."

2 Peter 1:19-21: "Men impelled by the Holy Spirit have spoken under God's influence."

Hymn Tuesday Morning Week II, "This Day God Gives Me" includes the words: "This day God sends me...wisdom as guide...Your lips are speaking, friend at my side."

Hymn Friday, Morning Prayer Week II "Speak to the soul of all the human race...Defeat our Babel with your Pentecost."

Antiphon Saturday Morning Prayer, Week II: "Let us listen to the voice of God..."

Saturday Morning Prayer Week II Canticle Antiphon: Lord, guide our feet into the way of peace."

Hymn Friday Week III Morning Prayer: "As we worship grant us vision, till your love's revealing light, till the height and depth and greatness, dawns upon our human sight...stirring us to faithful service, your abundant life to share."

Common of Holy Men, Morning Prayer Responsory: In the depth of his heart, the law of God is his guide...."

Prayer, Office of Readings, Saturday, Tenth Week in Ordinary Time: "God of wisdom and love, source of all good, send your Spirit to teach us our truth and guide our actions..."

St. Augustine, from Office of Readings June 26: "If I lack either the time or ability to study the implications of so profound a mystery, he who speaks within you even when I am not here will teach you better."

Some other reflections on the nature of these locutions:

When we read in Scripture in Acts about the gifts of the Holy Spirit, of which teaching is one, we may assume this means only teachings arrived at in the usual way by analysis of Scripture and Tradition, but the context could also suggest that these teachings could have been more infused knowledge. A Methodist Scripture scholar in my Christian Writing Group, Dr. Pat Looper, pointed out that her research shows that each of the prophets in the Old Testament is relating what God wants us to hear but in their own individual voice.

June 6, 2008
Receptivity

Holy Spirit: There is so much We wish to show you each moment. Right now, you hear the birds chirping outside the window and each picture on your wall glows with the meanings they have conveyed to you – some for 45 years. Don't you see that these unexpected post-60th birthday years are expanding your tight little soul?

We understand how hard it is to release into a more contemplative way of life for those who have been so active. So we offer you less and more busy times; we let you see the contrast, each mode with its pluses and minuses. The goal, always, that all may be received and given in peace and love. Look forward each day with joy and hope to the Mass and your quiet prayer time, for this is where you, in a focused way, let Us "melt and mold you, then fill you and use you," as your song goes. It is your receiving time. Humbly offer to Us those snarled up moments where you don't see your way forward. Wool is still useful after it is unraveled of knots. Bring those knots to Us in trust.

"For those who love God all things work for the good." (Romans 8;28)

June 7, 2008
Surrender

Holy Spirit: Everything. Yes, surrender everything to Us, because We are your real future. Do you see how your cats, even though they want to go out the door to a wider world, wait cautiously just outside the open door to check things out. Much more so do you look upward to heaven but then cringe backward shading your eyes from the sun. Surrender seems supine, but is really a courageous leap into the better but less known. You could practice surrendering each day, not just as a set prayer you could do making the motions of surrender but not the act of surrender. Instead make a real act of surrender many times a day. Ask your angel to help you.

Think of surrender as a dancer's leap. You stay in the air longer and longer and one day you don't come down. That is the end and the beginning.

(When going through these messages now in the year 2019, I am reciting the famous Novena of Surrender Prayer of Dom Dolindo. Google them.)

June 9, 2008
Surviving

Holy Spirit: You are torn between the instinct of survival and the desire to leave this world. As Mary Magdalene clung to the feet of Jesus after the resurrection and He said, "Do not touch me," she would have wanted to be raised in the Ascension clinging to His feet. But Peter tried to flee from martyrdom, and Jesus had to ask Him "Quo vadis?" When it is time for you to leave the earth, We will do it in you. Until then We let the survival instinct push you through the obstacles in life that otherwise might daunt you. Each morning is a sort of resurrection from the nightly death of your powers. Part of surrender is accepting this rhythm in your body/soul humanness. "Behold the handmaid of the Lord." That prayer of Mary is so perfect. See how she is clinging onto the Angel of the Annunciation, to Me, the Holy Spirit, who will conceive in her, and by pledging the future in her surrender, clinging to the Jesus, conceived in her, whom she will serve. So must you, in the morning self-offering, bind heaven and earth by choosing to survive not for earthly goals only, but surviving to do God's will "on earth as it is in heaven." (Matthew 6:10)

Are you seeing how the themes of each of these messages are joined? And, yes, as you suspect, they are linked to themes in each day's liturgical readings.

Courage!

June 11, 2008
The Future

Holy Spirit: You think of the future as a road already laid out that you must walk on. Rather, all the decisions of every person pave the road. May the pavement not have the imprint of a brutal, heavy boot. See how different paths look, the ones that are planted with the flowers of goodness! Without peril, the bare feet of a small child can walk on such a road. You cling to the news reports to be ready for the future. Do you ever see in these reports a picture of Jesus and hear His words, "follow Me"? But His feet lead straight to Calvary. Rather than follow behind Him, you would prefer to touch Him lightly when your paths cross. We want you to see the ultimate future as resurrected life so that you will run behind the Savior.

Sing as you run! "I have run the race; I have finished the course." (2 Timothy 4:7)

June 11, 2008 3 AM
Breaking Through

Holy Spirit: You observe around you graveyards of the dreams of others. You can choose between ridicule and grief. You can train a critical eye on defects to score points, or you can weep for those whose plans have crashed under the weight of their defects. Which path is right? The critic's path is justified. Didn't Jesus scathingly condemn the evils choking his country? This He did to make room for a new way that was harder but better. He also wept for those trapped themselves and manipulating others in power strategies. He wanted to gather the great and the weak under His wings to rescue them. The breakthrough is both deeper and higher than the bleak alternatives between which you think you have to choose (in your daily decisions). Do the beatitudes look like a plan for success in the world? The breakthrough is in the heart. Ask Us moment by moment to give you the love to see through all exterior evils into the disillusioned hearts of others. Is that not how We used Our followers to win your heart?

"Forgive us our trespasses as we forgive those who trespass against us." (Matthew 6:12)

June 12, 2008
Waiting to See

Holy Spirit: You want to pre-judge situations to flee from the pain of disappointment. But in this way, you cut off what is not full grown, or, as Jesus said, you "pull out the wheat with the chaff." We would like you to be willing to wait more to see what We have planted in souls that might need something from you. Every possibility is doomed if success is measured by a perfect score in reaching only one person's goals. Do children drop out of team sports unless they are the star players? Not if they love the game.

So do what you love, and bring along as many as respond for as long as they wish. Have gratitude for what comes that is good, but less measurement during the process. See how tense it makes you when you measure each activity every day? Trust in Us that We will draw you in and lead you out of the situations that come along. Loosen your grip. We have given you models such as St. Paul and St. Teresa of Avila who went many places and tried many things.

June 14, 2008
The Promised Land

Holy Spirit: The promised land is a prophecy, a dream, a rest stop, a foretaste, and finally your eternal home. All of it is Our gift, and you open the gift and enjoy it when you are willing to dwell in it. How can you enjoy the promised land if you are more like a looter rushing through the land, dragging on your back more than you can carry? In the Eucharist, Mother Church gives you the bread from heaven, a miniature form for the Eternal who entered time. In Confession, the priest, your travel agent so to speak, rids you of the excess baggage you took on in fear and greed. In each moment, through the lesser gifts of life on earth, We want to expand your hearts. Please notice.

June 14, 2008
Islands of Peace

Holy Spirit: In war, unconditional surrender leads to a time of peace. In a similar way, when many of you have been struggling within yourselves, you can give up all your ways of trying to win, and then We can enter and bring a time of peace. Remember how often Jesus says, "Be not afraid" and "Peace be with you."

It is not that We want to see you humiliated in your battles with yourselves and others. It is that there is no real winning on the human fields of battle you create, despite the beauty of your flags. We want to bury the dead and something new and unexpected rises from the ashes. The resurrection of Jesus: What is important is that it happened, not your analysis of how. So, too, in those little resurrections of hope after bitter tears. What is important is that you are there on a small island of peace. Take it in.

"Peace be with you." (John 20;19)

June 15, 2008
The Prize

Holy Spirit: What do you really want, my children? More? More life, more joy, more love, more success? Your whole being is created to want more. You are not like rocks in the sun. You are always in motion toward some prized reward – short and long-term wishes and goals.

It is a sort of race. It tires you out always running toward prizes, but to sit still also tires you out. You can experience this as a rhythm of work and Sabbath, running to rest; resting to run again. What do We really want for Our children? More life, more joy, more love, more of the right kind of success. (Author's Note: I thought this meant how success is being a good sport sometimes vs. winning a game.)

Jesus told you before He left this earth that He would send Me to guide you. The guide book is the Bible and the teachings of our Church. Also, Me speaking in each of your hearts. The light shines through. We look for docile, eager students who we can teach to run toward the good and also to rest in it. We have chosen you; do you want to pledge yourself to Us?

"I have finished the race." (2 Timothy 4:7)

June 16, 2008
Pace and Openness

Holy Spirit: Imagine a sight-seeing procession. Ideally, it is timed for the right amount of contact with what is to be viewed. The tourists are not jostled quickly past the most important sites. Rural life was paced by nature: dawn, midday sun, twilight, nightfall, seasons. There was ample time to absorb the nature of trees and animals and weather in the midst of the work cycle. Think of cooking (as an example of absorbing the nature of each food). Think also of the pace of monastic hours of prayer.

In your era, you think instead of spirituality as leaping out of time, out of nature, into the eternal. You think of being saved from the realities you have made, into our eternal now. More Catholic, universal, is a rhythm of the created with the Uncreated, in and out, out and in, like breath. When you release yourself into Us in prayer, we fill you and then send you back into your world to be open to it and transform it. The pace is liturgical, not rushed.

"There will be a new heaven and a new earth." (Revelation 21:1)

June 17, 2008
Acceptance?

Holy Spirit: Your sins nail others to the cross. Obvious are the victims when the sins are theft, scorn, babies torn from their mother's wombs, terrorized innocents in wars. Less obvious are the victims when they are in complicity, as when the victims of lust short-change each other willingly. And is the exploited laborer who wants the job not still a victim? The victims don't always look like Christ on the cross, but they feel the nails in their hearts. How can you both fight sin, your own and those of others, and yet accept having to live in a world that is full of sin?

Picture a fleeing mob coming upon a launching pad. They see battered but viable helicopters descending to rescue them. Some, wounded in battle, slink away rejecting helping hands. Most let themselves be carried on board. Once safely on board, they spy their pursuers on the ground. Some throw things out of the planes to hit their enemies, but one calls out: "Surrender! If you surrender, after we land in safety we will send back rescue planes for you, too."

Which choice will you make? Can you see your enemy as one as desperate as you? You are not called to accept sin, but "to love the sinner."

(Author's Note: As a member of the board of directors at Flynn House [a group home for men addicted to alcohol and drugs], I thought I should know more about what the AA meetings are actually like. I was astounded. Here were all these "tough guys" – quite a number on motorcycles, coming in and being so warm to each other and open and honest and needy of each other. I thought, my God, does it take reaching a bottom that low before men can relate in a heart-felt manner to each other? I am now thinking that these locutions from the Holy Spirit are supposed to be related to my experiences during the day, partly to train me through deeper insights. So I am including the context of some of them where that context seems relevant.)

Pride of Life

"For all that is in the world, the lust of the flesh and the lust of the eye and the pride of life, is not of the Father but of the world." (1 John 2)

Holy Spirit: You like to see energy in people: in sport, dance, building, climbing, bringing powerful music out of an organ. In nature you like to see the power of the ocean or in a tiger. Adam and Eve were full of such life. Then you see the bad side of power: arrogance, dominance, Cain killing Abel. In every situation after the fall, there are the two sides: the happy joy of life and the bad pride of life of feeling superior. That pride must be crushed before We can make the "new man in Christ."

One must lose the bad pride of life, for instance, because of ill-fortune or the grim consequences of sin, before one can be molded as soft dough into a person who can love and show the need for being loved. To pray is to acknowledge that your life-force was not and is not enough to bring the happiness you crave. Through your surrender to Us in prayers, We can transform the bad pride of life into energy for building the kingdom of God, on earth as it is in heaven.

June 18, 2008
Leaning

Holy Spirit: It takes defeat for most men to become humble and willing to accept the help of God and of other men. For most women, it takes disillusionment to lean less on men and stand upright in the strength of the Spirit. Hand in hand, walking with God, the redeemed men and women can go forward. Hand in hand is not one dominating and the other leaning. Hand in hand is the ideal. You see it in Mary and Joseph. Think of the journey to Egypt. Joseph had been broken in his pride by the people thinking the baby in Mary's womb was not his. Mary could not lean on Joseph during his time of uncertainty. Now, together, they go off to Egypt, a new land for them, hand in hand with the God-man, little Jesus.

Between the unredeemed and the redeemed is a long process of life together for you men and women with all the conflicts. You cannot go forward without the essential element of forgiveness. Parents want to be as gods to their children. The children take all their strength, drink up all their love. All that time they need to be and love in the divine Father, and in a different way, in Mary, their spiritual mother. Children need to grow up; that is upward, toward their heavenly destiny. When they have outgrown their intense neediness, they don't lean, but join hands with you. The way is strewn with crosses, but leads to the promised land.

June 20, 2008
Give to the Poor

(It seemed as if I dreamt in Spanish to "evitar" the "chip:34" and give to the poor. I awoke with a sense of fear. There is a conspiracy theory that claims that before the end of the world, the Anti-Christ will make everyone insert a chip in their foreheads in order to prove identity, and that this will be used to tyrannize us.)

Holy Spirit: Do not be afraid. Cling to the Church and give to the poor. The "chip" is a symbol of the world and fear of loss. Those who have Us as their focus don't need to fear. We want you to be a "light" at the top of the mountain. We have prepared you for a long time. Those who want to be poor are not desperate if a change in life-style becomes prevalent. You can start now to do things in more basic ways. We will help you. Ask about each thing you buy or undertake: Is this necessary? Savor what you have in each moment.

"Behold, I make all things new." (Rev 21:5)

June 21, 2008
Lightness

Holy Spirit: The more insecure you feel, the more heavy-handed you become as you grab onto what you want. When it is people you are grabbing onto, they will often resist to avoid becoming prey, entrapped, used. This is why quiet prayer time is a necessity. Can you see how much lighter is the approach to life of those who are more secure? The climber with a sure guide finds the right place to put the foot and from that secure place can reach out and up with a lighter hold.

There are many ways of explaining this: the Eastern concept of detachment or a phrase like "Let go, let God." Now, don't become heavy-hearted thinking about how insecure you still are! When you feel insecure, what you have to do is grip tightly onto Us. Since We are usually invisible, you have to do this through prayer. For those with many tasks, this can be done with little prayers throughout the day and then longer times as possible. For those of you with ample time, the insecurity of so many possibilities could bring you often to Us for longer times of restful peace. From Us, you can move more lightly into the next moments of your day. "My peace I give unto you, not as the world gives." (John 14:27)

105

(A quote from Lily Tomlin! "Why is it when we talk to God, we are said to be praying but when God talks to us, we're said to be schizophrenic?")

June 22, 2008
Wisdom

Holy Spirit: Wisdom without patience leaves out love. What good is it to understand more and more about the global scene and the people around you and about yourself if you don't have the patient love to overcome the disgust that comes from bitter truths? Honor those who doggedly work moment by moment to learn and apply and wait. Remember the images of patient farmers Jesus gave you. To surrender your hearts to God and surrender to God those you love, which should include all humanity, is to recognize that only His love can bridge the gap between truth and realization.

In some past eras and in some countries now, the perception of injustice led and leads into immediate impulses to vengeance. In your times, often impatience leads to the so-called quick fix for all frustrations by any method near at hand, from breaking the law to abortion. Person by person and person to person, you need to learn to come into divine wisdom and live that wisdom in patient love. "In your patience you will save your souls."

June 23, 2008
Unity and Truth

Holy Spirit: You are concerned that the Transition (A term used in the visions and locutions of a friend of mine. I thought it might have to do with the hoped-for Triumph of the Immaculate Heart.) will bring people from different religions into a false unity to the sacrifice of truth. That is because you are looking for external unity. What we are bringing about is a more spiritual unity of all who have been open to letting Us invade their hearts. When people of many religions and nations visit the Pope, he doesn't proclaim that there is only one true Church and they must enter. He tries to reach into their hearts by understanding and gifts so that they feel loved.

One day, all the saved will know God to be Father, Son and Holy Spirit and will be one universal worshipping body, but the way we will bring this about and the way it will look will not be as you picture it now.

Think of the painting in your (parish) Church of Christ, the Guru. It is not a picture of an Indian holy man worshipping a cross. It is Jesus showing Himself in the form that an Indian would understand.

Or think of the many images of Mary in the apparitions of the different nations. She doesn't have to look like a Jewish woman of the Old Testament to be true. An Eastern Catholic Church united to Rome looks more like an orthodox church than a Roman church. Mother Teresa looked more like an Indian woman than like a traditional Catholic nun.

Meanwhile, We want to give you the experiences and the gifts to be a light shining in the darkness until the day the light and the darkness will be permanently severed. "Speak the truth with love," (Ephesians 4:15) and you will kindle the flame.

June 24, 2008
Fear

Holy Spirit: You often wake up fearful. It is part of your nature as a contingent being, always in need. It is part of living among strangers with unknown motives. How do we work to change fear into trust? Before the Transition, we trained you in your morning offering to turn to Our invisible presence. In giving your day to Us, you would be reminded of the purpose of your life and how your emotions could be brought under the control of Our providence, and will. Throughout the day in prayer, you linked your quaking or tired or grateful hearts to Us. Those who received daily the Body and Blood of Jesus were strengthened by His real presence coming right into their bodies. With daily contrition and the sacrament of penance (weekly in the past), you allowed Us to take away the debilitating consequences of sin such as the fear that leads to and issues from hate.

Till the end of the world, these will be our fundamental ways to be closer to you and overcome your fear. You will be able to see Us and feel Our presences as a constant, each in your own way. You will be less likely to fall into the abyss of your own weaknesses.

June 25, 2008
Personal Spirituality

Holy Spirit: Christian doctrine is objective and unassailable. Though it is ultimately about the salvation of each person, it is not focused on the specific personality of each of you. Scripture, by contrast, includes stories with specific words and actions of individuals. You will notice that it is full of risk. David has to trust that God wants to make use of his training in stoning wild beasts to help him defeat Goliath. He risks his life on his trust that it is God's will that he step forward.

In your personal history, you have times where the risks you took failed in your purpose. A small child tries to show love for a parent with a gift that is ridiculed; a man or woman reveals love for a person who rejects him or her. As a result, you can become wary of self-revelation. Your way of being with Us, instead of being child-like and free, can become overly formal.

There is balance when you have in each day some perfectly-formed liturgical prayer, but then also, an ever-flowing current of personal lifting of your hearts in trust to Us and to our family of Mary, angels, and saints. There is healing when you are elevated above random prayer into the universal rhythm of liturgy. There is healing, also, in believing that We who created you to be an individual person cherish your endearing ways of showing your love and receiving Our love. Think of Mary Magdalene plunging through the ridicule of the Pharisees to anoint the feet of Jesus with her hair.

Singing in worship is so important with each person's voice harmonizing with the others in praise. Also, when those with the gift of tongues pray, each one's words are different, but they blend in song.

If you recall, I am called "the comforter." There is comfort in losing yourself in the throng in public formal prayer. There is also comfort in curling up into Our embrace in littleness in personal prayer. Pray to be free of every fear that keeps you from fullness.

"I will send the Holy Spirit, the comforter."

June 26, 2008
Light Shines in Darkness

Holy Spirit: Some days, dark powers seem triumphant. You thought you had found a place of security and find instead darkness and danger. It makes you want to hide. The Apostles on Palm Sunday felt triumphant. By Good Friday most fled and hid. Now it is your turn. Sometimes We tell you to flee, but more often We want you, whatever the price, to stay as a lampstand for Our light. You are to speak the truth, not with hate, but with love. If not you, who? Can you sense that your own words are stronger since you have been receiving these messages? Often, when you feel you cannot win, that is the time when We can win, even if our victory is not visible. Was Our victory visible when Jesus was crucified? Only a few saw the light bursting through the darkness, but those few were enough for Us to use to spread the light throughout the whole world.

June 27, 2008
"The Greatest of These is Love"

Holy Spirit: God has led each of you through different paths to different treasures. You can come to love a value or virtue in such a way that you become not only its champion but also its defender, and then can set in almost a spirit of rivalry. St. Paul wrote of the different gifts of the Spirit, culminating with the blazing proclamation that the greatest of these is love. Can you see that the quality of one small deed of love having its source in divine love is "the pearl of great price?" (Matthew 13:46)

It is not a matter of teeth-gritting decisions to overcome your resistance to sacrifice. Rather by sincerity of response to Our love for you, you let Us overcome the resistance to sacrifice. Humble contrition for failure keeps your hearts from closing up in defensive rationalizations of selfishness. Gradually your heart is enlarged. In the end, there will be no stopping the flow of love.

June 28, 2008

Holy Spirit: "On the top of the mountain, "no-thing." (an allusion to the famous saying of St. John of the Cross: On top of the mountain, nothing.)

The air is thinner: no smog. You are lighter: less attachments. Do you see that being "we" with Us you are better?

more free

not so shaky

not so angry

not so tired

less closed in with your wounds

more close into other's hearts?

We call it "the Transition."

June 29, 2008

(At the Prayer Meeting, I immediately associated the radiant mysticism of the leaders and some others with the term "ecstatic union" Mary gave us concerning the Transition.)

Holy Spirit: There is pathos in hope. To wish for what is not immediately present seems to court failure. Disappointment is humiliating. See how staunch was the hope of Mary and John and the few others standing under the Cross! Coming to Church is an act not only of faith but of hope. You hope that responding to Our promise will bring you and others one day to heaven. Each little prayer for each other is a banner of hope. What about hope for yourselves and each other here on earth? Pessimism can be self-protective, judgmental. It can close you to grace. But naïve hope is a denial of obstacles to success within and without.

The Christian is to see the seeds of God amidst the brambles; to applaud the spring rains and the signs of growth that follow. Can you hear Us begging you to hope? How could We lead the saints into martyrdom if We didn't know that We could fulfill their hope?

"....and even if it die..." (John 12:24)

June, 2008
Power

Holy Spirit: You love power and you fear power. It is the human condition. Jesus tries to teach you something to transcend human ways of understanding, as in "behold the lilies of the field," or the temple veil is rent by an earthquake, but also by the drops of His blood or the child as the symbol of the kingdom.

The words of St. Paul speak of Christian virtue as the power to do good. Your minds must be on the Gospel, the good news. Scanning the horizon for the bad news brings the illusion of the power to resist, but resolves nothing, for there are always powerful enemies without and within that threaten you. The augmented power you feel in the joining of hands is a symbol of the different type of power. The images in Scripture of the end of the world symbolize the defeat of purely natural power. Christ's resurrected body doesn't defeat the Romans but defeats the laws of gravity as it ascends.

Grab His feet!

July 1, 2008
Being Drawn In

Holy Spirit: We, the source of your being, want to draw you always further in. Grace can be for the purpose of giving you extra energy to do Our will on earth. Think of St. Paul and other missionaries. Think of a Christian's daily life of work for others. Grace is the energy for good action, but it is also the power to enter in to Our realm. You rest in Us and breathe in fresh air so you return to your work with new energy. Watch this in those you think are close to Us. Can you see when their faces reveal more light? Can you feel more tenderness in their glance or touch? The seed is hard, the fruit is soft.

"You shall go from grace to grace, from glory to glory." (2 Corinthians 3:18)

July 2, 2008
Written Words and Persons

(On the Feast of St. Peter and Paul, our priest, Fr. Ken Whittington, gave an incisive sermon to us in this Bible Belt area of North Carolina. Quoting Jesus making Peter the Rock on which He would build His church, Fr. Ken said, "He didn't say on this book I will build My church. The church assembled the New Testament gradually. Of course, he added, the Bible is the Word of God, but it is not the rock.)

Holy Spirit: You read about Jesus naming Peter the Rock in the sacred book, but in the earliest days of the Church the people (who had not seen Jesus themselves when He was on earth) heard about Jesus from the mouths of people, the apostles, the disciples. The resurrected Jesus spoke to Mary Magdalene, to Peter, and to Thomas personally. The written word is a means, not a substitute for persons. People change and wound, so you can come to prefer written words to people, thinking words hold still. We use the words of truth to reach your minds and hearts such as the words of the Creed. But the Word that became flesh was a person; the second Person of the Trinity, and then a person on earth.

When the body dies, you will not see a book but a Person, your savior. Heaven will not be a library, but the communion of persons. Because of what He saw and felt in a personal encounter, St. Thomas Aquinas thought the words in his books were but straw. We are not asking you to throw away all books with written words. Are not these

111

messages sent to become written words? But We do not want you to cling to them as if they were your salvation? Each single moment of contact in loving presence with Us or with any human person can be for you an opening of the doors of heaven; an opening toward the ecstatic union.

After all, new human persons do not come from words but from the "ecstatic union" of two persons. Is not the Trinity an ecstatic union of Persons?

July 3, 2008
Setting Forth on a Sea More Vast

Holy Spirit: You long for larger horizons. At the same time, you rush back to the cozy safety of your homes. This is a natural in and out of human life on earth.

For your minds there is a joy in opening to wider views, but then you can become lost in speculation and need to come home to the fundamental truths. In the Church, we present to you the vista of an unknown but gleaming heaven and then gather you into your well-known parish settings with the one table of the sacrifice, finally giving you what is as safe as one Eucharistic host. In this out-and-in rhythm, you suddenly feel bewildered. You need to echo the words of Jesus on the Cross: "Into Your hands I commend my spirit."

Children laugh more than adults because they have more trust, but the benign smile of an old one tells of long-tested trust and abiding hope. (The smile of Pope Benedict XVI?) The sailors knew to trust Mary, Star of the Sea.

July 4, 2008
Intensity

Holy Spirit: We want you to be intense in a way that attracts rather than frightens. We want an intensity of love, not of pseudo-power. People were not afraid of Jesus, Mary, and Joseph. They were drawn by the intensity of their love. So also with the saints. It seems to you paradoxical that to become more intense in this loving way, you have to become more relaxed in your prayer. Prayer of presence is not tense but receptive. This is because supernatural love that comes into you and radiates from you is not tense. Tension comes from fear.

Our love is intense because it is person to person, but it is relaxed because it is a response to what is of unchangeable value: your created being and what We have created in the being of those you encounter. Supernatural intensity is as rhythmic as music. Tension, by contrast, is jerky, as you try to coerce others into fitting into some plan you have created to allay fear; for example, fear of loneliness. So do not begrudge Us the time of receptive prayer. The ecstatic union depends upon your willingness to come out of your habitual state of defensive planning. Refreshed by Our intense tender love for you, you will be better able to direct rays of love into the hearts of others.

Try!

July 5, 2008
Silence

Holy Spirit: With what words can We teach you the limits of words? We want to teach you not a dull silence but a rich silence; the silence that comes from going out of yourself into ecstatic union with Us and our creation. Tedious chatter comes from your enemy: fear. You try to ward off fear, ultimately fear of death, through wordy plans. Since corpses are silent, you prove to yourselves that you are alive by hearing your own voices. Speech as response is better; more musical. You hear a request, pick up a concern, sense a need. Your voiced response signifies you are ready with helpful love. Your tongue cries out against the threat of such seeming restriction. You ask if I would condemn the joys of self-expression?

Always you want to justify excess by reference to the evil of its opposite: poverty. We treasure your spontaneous personal voices. What we wish to tame is the scattered noises of your anxiety. Try for just awhile slowing down and questioning what you want to say. Favor words of communion with Us; words of praise of beauties large as the sky, small as a flower; words of thanksgiving; words of humble need. Reject words of anger; words of complaint; words of critique; words of prodding. One day your song will blend into Our song.

(Beware) "The tongue is a fire...set on fire by hell." (James 3:6)

July 6, 2008
Poured Out

Holy Spirit: It is safe inside the bottle, the libation slowly gaining flavor and strength. The interior life grows in darkness. Then comes the time to let Us bring you out to be served, tested, tasted, relished, or perhaps, spit out! We waste nothing. Think of the angels saving the blood pouring out of the side of your Savior on the crucifix.

Mary's and your consent to Our plan is at first without boundaries. The specifics of Our plan unfold. At each unexpected turn, We leave you free to take back your consent. Appalled, Peter cried out: "I know not that man!" Your weaknesses become part of Our plan. How many find in Peter's tears the impetus to their own repentance! The risen Jesus came right through the locked doors of His hidden disciples. He was eager to reassure them. He will anoint them before leading them forth, themselves, to be poured out. Take courage. Let us lead you into the unknown future.

"The light shines in the darkness and the darkness shall not overcome it." (John 1:5)

July 7, 2008
Results

Holy Spirit: You think of results as direct effects of causes. We think more of radiation of power as in light. When you don't see results as you try to witness to Our love, you are disappointed. We are not disappointed because We are sending love to others through you. The light shines through even the darkness in you that makes you so ashamed. The darkness in you does block those you witness to from accepting you or accepting your concrete plans for them. As it were, they throw away the package, you, and grab what is inside (Our love). All you see is how they reject the package, and you feel discouraged. You don't see them in the home in their hearts cherishing the gift. If this were not true, how could 12 men who were martyred "cause" the conversion of peoples throughout the whole world?

I hear the sceptic in you shrugging this off. With the cause and effect mentality, you think this result came more from conquest than from grace. That is the dark side. But because We are Love, Our rays come into the hearts of all who open to Us no matter what the circumstances.

"I am the light of the world."

July 8, 2008
Microcosm

(Note: Words in parentheses are Ronda's explanations)

Holy Spirit: We want you to learn how to see the All in the small. This is not pantheism (the theory that all creatures are God) or sentimentality (a fatuous cooing over the sweet), as you might fear. It has to do with the imago Dei, with omnipresence, with symbols, with ecstatic union.

Think of

- all the notes in a symphony rushing toward the final triumphant chord;
- the kiss of bride and groom at a wedding;
- the smile of a baby: the first to be seen by the parents;
- each Mass encapsulating every Mass;
- the end, when the barriers break down between the religions of the world, all will become one, not in some false blurring synthesis, but in a mighty ecstatic union where the partial will rush toward the full.

July 9, 2008
Convergence

Holy Spirit: The closer you get to heaven, the more earthly division distresses you. You see no way to overcome it, whether it be in the realm of the political or the ecclesial. These divisions are long entrenched, coming as they do from real sins of the past. Healing will come through grace. You can cooperate in making openings for grace by avoiding denunciation in favor of understanding the reasons for the dividing stances. Imagination can help. Think of small children learning fear and hate as necessary for self-protection.

Let yourself notice the unexpected that comes when someone leaps over the division in a gesture of solidarity. Don't you want to be one who, with Our help, can make those kinds of leaps? Start by noticing in yourself the impulses to fear and hate and how they come up in the moment you are thwarted in the smallest goal. Can you see that quietly accepting the jolt to your will and working through the problem for the best solution, feels peaceful? It prevents you from hasty, harsh, blame with the retaliation that cements division.

Humble forgiveness put you and others on the same plane. And then, with the same people or similar ones, at another time, there can be a convergence of needs and helps. It is not a matter of "figuring out," but of releasing it into Our hands and then responding to Our prompts.

"In the world it is impossible, but nothing is impossible for God."

"Blessed are the peacemakers."

July 10, 2008
Comfort

(I awoke during the night with a sense of motherly warmth: my mother's? Mary's? And then came this locution:)

Holy Spirit: The word has an ambiguous ring to you. The desire to be comforted can seem babyish, as if refusing the tough challenges of life in work or even sports. Yet the "giving of comfort" always sounds maternal in a positive way. To prepare you for heaven, then, We simultaneously wean you from too human a need for earthly comforts, and attach you to spiritual comfort.

What is spiritual comfort? It can come from Divine grace pouring into your souls, but it can also come from the hope of Our approval for your righteousness when you chose the good, often at some sacrifice. This comes from Our paternal justice.

From deprivation of human comfort, you can become closed or combative. Moderate human comforts are healing of this: good food, drink, the warmth of the sun. Surfeit of comforts makes you sluggish. All this is part of the drama of life. Part of heaven will be to know how it all worked. Will you let the richness of all these elements of life give you hope?

"We now see through a glass darkly."

July 11, 2008
Security

Holy Spirit: There is a good security. Think of "the house built on good foundations," being with people you trust because they are honest and responsible; sound investments, hard earned savings. This is good, but there is something better: the security of being saved by

God's all-understanding love. In this sense, mercy is safer than justice, for "who can ransom his own soul?" even with piles of merit?

St. Francis of Assisi called death "sister death." He understood death as a sort of trampoline to help you leap from your temporal securities into the security of God the Father's waiting arms. Judgment there will be, but no longer on your own fallible terms. So much of the gospel is about letting go of earthly security, the stocking up of barns for a non-existent future.

Come! Let yourself be saved.

July 12, 2008
Insight

Holy Spirit: Beware of circling around stale self-justifying thoughts. Such repetition is very different from the wholesome cycle of nature or the rhythm of daily activities which brings peace. Insight comes when you let the rays of Trinitarian light into the darkness of mind that comes with the Fall. The Gospels are full of parables about such breakthroughs: the Prodigal son; and encounters with real people such as the woman at the well.

The Good News According to _____ (your name) could be written about such moments of turning. In periods when your life is not in crisis, We try to give you insight through watching nature or casual encounters. The sky tells you of the infinite. The pleasure of a supermarket worker helping you find what you are looking for could give you insight into the goodness of inter-dependence. Favorite music lifts you above the tragic: a sign that you are not stuck in frustration but can transcend it. Simplicity of life should lead to less rush and pressure with more room to receive fresh insight. Even in physical pain, disappointment, or loss, open to the Spirit of Truth for unexpected light.

July 12, 2008
Cultures Blended and Transformed

(Of all the locutions in this series this one seems most like me writing rather than the Holy Spirit. On the other hand, it corresponds in many ways to the reading at the Mass for the 15th Sunday in Ordinary time which followed the locution, and of course, some of the ideas which seem like summaries of my own previous reflections on life could themselves have been inspired by the Holy Spirit. You can just take whatever you think is true and ruminate on it.)

Holy Spirit: You can rightly bemoan the violence of the history of peoples; of conquest; the blood of battle; the enslavement of peoples. How do We bring good out of all those sins that exploded out of the initial rupture of the peace of Eden? You can see this good in the fact of the tilma of Our Lady of Guadalupe (this is the miraculous and beautiful imprint of Mary's face on the robe of a Mexican during the time of the conquistadores which led to the conversion of millions of Mexicans). It is a noble, sorrowful, native face, yet she also appears as the transformation of Spanish culture. The craving for gold is transmuted into the prophesied gold of Revelation in the image of the woman clothed with the sun.

Can you see in the portrait of St. Paul in the Scripture the blending of the fierce Jewish obedience to God with the Roman vision of universality? In United States culture, out of the tragedy of slavery you see coming forth the Afro-American mode of love for Jesus which you hear in passionate gospel music. Now with the waves of immigration, you can see out of intense survival needs coming forth a fiery expression of desperation and gratitude for salvation penetrating the perennial universal (Catholic means universal), more serene rituals.

We don't will for you the miseries of evil in the tangled effects from the paths you took when you chose to listen to the Evil One rather than walk with your Father in the garden. It is from all of that tragedy that you are to be redeemed, saved, and a sign of redemption is the transfiguration of each people. Violence is a foretaste of hell; beauty a foretaste of heaven.

(Later, when I was "arguing" with the Holy Spirit that this all sounded too blunt, with not enough sense of the mystery of suffering that we cannot understand and can only accept because of the gift of faith, He seemed to add this example: The devil leads people to abortion, but the souls of the babies go into the lap of Mary.)

July 14, 2008

Signs of Awakening (This is from a Catholic 12-Step Reading)

1. We desired greater closeness to God but knew we could not bring this about by ourselves.

2. We became aware that God wished to be closer to us in the innermost recesses of our heart.

3. We sensed, saw, or heard God breaking through the barriers in us of sin, routine, and fear.

4. We found the Holy Spirit's presence more strongly reaching out to us in our individual and group prayer; in the liturgy, and in communion and reconciliation; to comfort and guide us.

5. We perceived Jesus, more and more, in the suffering hearts of others: those close to us and those less known. This gave us fresh impetus to try to overcome injustices of small and larger scale.

6. We found mercy in the kindness and goodness in the hearts of others for ourselves.

7. We saw God's hand more clearly in the beauty in nature, in human inventiveness, and in the arts.

8. We felt the embrace of Jesus and Mary in our worst physical and emotional pain. This enabled us better to forgive others and ourselves.

9. We believed and hoped more strongly, in spite of all our weaknesses and evils, in God's plan of love for the present and for eternity.

10. We experienced our beings expanding with greater joy, peace, trust, gratitude, and love.

July 15, 2008
"Nothing ventured, nothing gained."

Holy Spirit: Jesus warned you about hoarding; about a false sense of security for those who take no risks. Because He was the "Way, the Truth and the Life," He asked his children, his followers, to risk even death on a cross for a heaven they could not see. In spite of the evidence of the miracles, many followers, even the closest, chose flight over the risk of crucifixion. Can you blame them?

At certain moments in each of your lives, you come to a crossroads where the price of faith seems too great; everything to gain by being a spectator instead of a player...or so it can seem. How often Jesus chided the people for their lack of faith. This would be cruel unless He, Himself, had given them the evidence to make the leap. Hands are dragging you back to the safety of skepticism? Whose hands are waving to you from a better place on high?

(I thought of St. Paul – first totally skeptical to the point of persecuting and arranging for the death of Christians, but then converted by a vision only he saw.)

July 16, 2008
1,2,3, Go!

Holy Spirit: At a race or a performance, you train and train and train, and then it is upon you and you have to let go of everything else and rush into the act. We want you now to be decisively focused, not on a physical feat but for loving response. That is what poverty of spirit is about. Only when you are empty of your self-protective calculations can we fill you with our energies of love. But it is not as if you were a mere instrument or machine. It is precisely through your natural, freely-responding personality that We want to work.

- Think of a mother singing to her babe.
- Think of a carpenter smoothing a piece of wood.
- Think of St. Peter looking at the fish in the net and envisaging them as the means for the metaphor Jesus told him about catching men for the kingdom.
- Think of the people you call holy. Don't you feel in them this readiness to respond? Yet they are not tense, just truly present, and in their eyes you see their love.

It is all right if these words make you feel inadequate. That should lead you the more to welcome Us in prayer.

July 17, 2008
Watching and Waiting

Holy Spirit: In the light you see beautiful qualities in each other. These you want to embrace that you might have them always with you. Shortly afterwards, the shadows fall over the image and you see only what is dark, closed in, finally a mere outline. From this vision, dismayed, you recoil; reject. How can human love be steadfast if that is the only cycle? Who can survive such scrutiny? It would seem that only inertia would keep any of you together. Is our Christian call to love, then, no more than a pathetic fantasy? That would be to think only the perfect is real. That is one way of transcendence; one form of "God Alone is Enough." The disciples wanted to stay on top of the mountain with the transfigured Jesus, never to return to the city.

Another way to understand "God Alone is Enough", that We wish for you, is to cherish the sparks of the beautiful divine you see in each other, and forgive the limitations and betrayals. Then, wait for your mercy for them, and theirs for you, to show you a redeemed goodness. That We call the coming of the kingdom, the transition. When "God Alone is Enough," you can love each other with tenderness instead of thirst.

July 18, 2008
Transparency

Holy Spirit: (During the Retreat Fr. Ken said that a spiritual master used to give this method of following the injunction in the New Testament to pray constantly. Here is a paraphrase: In every minute take one second to lift your heart to God; in every hour take a minute to lift your heart to God; in every day take an hour to lift your heart to God; in every week take a day to lift your heart to God; in every year take a week to lift your heart to God. I snapped back with, "So, do you actually do this, Fr. Ken?" I thought he would say something funny in reply, but he looked at us with the same absolutely solemn expression he has at Mass and said, "Yes, more or less.")

You humans develop a teasing and self-deprecating banter to cover your jockeying for power or your shy fear of rejection. All the more, how beautiful it is when We succeed in overcoming all that to make openings between you where, unexpectedly, there it is: the voice, the eyes, simply revealing your deepest selves. That is what was meant when we taught you that you must be vulnerable to be able to heal. Such transparency happens. It is grace. You cannot make it happen. It is a foretaste of heaven where there will be no concealment, and there will be no reason to fear. Can you imagine the power that was in the transparent contact when Jesus looked at a person directly in the eyes before performing a miracle, or when He said "It is I?" Great artists know how to convey that focused transparency when they paint the Holy Face.

Look and learn!

July 19, 2008
In His Footsteps

(I have a grandson, Nicholas, who looks at lot like Jim Caviezel as Jesus in *The Passion*.

One day, it happened that Nicholas was staggering under the weight of a large couch he was dragging from the back of his van. His body assumed the posture of Jesus carrying His cross.)

My grandson Nicholas.

Holy Spirit: You make the Stations of the Cross as a devotion often with contemporary words to relate them to your own lives. Still, you do not always see that you are treading in the footsteps of Jesus when it is your own suffering:

- the agony of impending physical or emotional pain;
- the being under the will of powerful strangers;
- the horror of submitting to unjust judgment;
- present inescapable pain;
- the falling from a status of popular acclaim to being an object of criticism or ridicule;
- the finality of loss by death, literal or figurative.

Of a sudden, We help you identify with Him on this bloody road. For a second you see that you are not alone. If you stay with that identification, you can become a true Christian. Then you will feel also in your own bones many resurrections.

(I was so happy to see the Holy Father, Pope Benedict, expressing so clearly in his words what these messages mean to me. "This is why I think that the most important thing is that we ourselves remain, so to speak, within the radius of the Holy Spirit's breath, in contact with Him. Only if we are continually touched within by the Holy Spirit, if He dwells in us, will it be possible for us to pass Him on to others. Then he gives us the imagination and creative ideas about how to act, ideas that cannot be planned but are born from the situation itself, because it is there that the Holy Spirit is at work. Thus, the first point: we ourselves must remain within the radius of the Holy Spirit's breath. St. John's Gospel tell us that after the Resurrection the Lord went to his disciples, breathed upon them and said: 'Receive the Holy Spirit.' This is a parallel to Genesis, where God breathes on the mixture he made with the dust from the earth and it comes to life and becomes man. Then man, who is inwardly darkened and half dead, receives Christ's breath anew and it is this breath of God that gives his life a new dimension, that gives him life with the Holy Spirit. We can say, therefore, that the Holy Spirit is the breath of Jesus Christ and we, in a certain sense, must ask Christ to breathe on us always, so that His breath will become alive and strong and work upon the world. This means that we must keep close to Christ.... And of course, first of all in the blessed sacrament of the Eucharist in which He comes to us and enters us and is, as it were, amalgamated with us. Then, however, also in the sacrament of penance, which always purifies us, which washes away the grime that daily life deposits in us... All this must determine the shape that our day takes in such a way that it becomes structured, a day in which God has access to us all the time, in which we are in continuous contact with Christ and in which, for this very reason, we are continuously receiving the breath of the Holy Spirit. If we do this, if we are not too lazy, undisciplined or sluggish, then something happens to us: the day acquires a form and in it our life itself acquires a form and this light will shine from us without us having to give it much thought or having to adopt a 'propagandist' — so to speak — way of acting: It comes automatically because it mirrors our soul. To this I would then add a second dimension that is logically linked with the first: If we live with Christ we will also succeed in human things. Indeed, faith does not only involve a supernatural aspect, it rebuilds man, bringing him back to his humanity...It is based precisely on the natural virtues: honesty, joy, the willingness to listen to one's neighbor, the ability to forgive, generosity, goodness and cordiality among people.")

July 20, 2008
Comfort at the Core

Holy Spirit: In the body/soul unity of your personhood, you find both physical and emotional comfort through the assuagement of your needs, when you are warm and fed and also feel safe. We usually have you grow in the shelter of the family. We lead some saints to toss aside such physical comfort to prove to the human race that there is something greater than "bread alone." But most of you We lead slowly step by step to enjoy a sense of well-being in the Spirit through music, art, being surrounded by the arms of the Church building. We bring you into the Sacraments where mysteriously through the visible you can be saved and comforted by Our invisible presence. We wean you from total immersion in physical comforts toward the separation of soul and body at death. Our plan is not for you to feel terrified, but rather by greater and greater union with the Holy Family to be comforted in your souls as you make the transition. To show you that one day the body will be restored to you transfigured, we give you homey images of Jesus' resurrected body such as cooking fish for His followers and promising them that one day they will find themselves in mansions prepared for them by Him where there will be no more tears.

July 21, 2008
"The Twinkling of an Eye"

Holy Spirit: We give you enough of a view of the distant shore so that you will be willing to pull with your oars toward the goal. You are often so tired that all you want is to give up. We understand. Can you see that these messages are a glimpse of the shoreline? Of course, tired sailors have to pace themselves. When you overexert yourselves you are more likely to collapse. Pacing yourselves means often resting your oars and gazing at the shore. You do that when you stop to pray even for an instant. We value such prayer more than you do. We want you to receive Our encouragement as a sportsman turns for a moment in the direction of the coach. Do you really believe in the words of the great champion, St. Paul, that one day all will be changed in the twinkling of an eye? Would We give you "a stone instead of a fish?" It will help you to sing as you row. If you listen up you will hear Us singing with you.

July 22, 2008
Impasse

Holy Spirit: The natural way in battle is fight or flight. It is perilous to transport that pattern into spiritual warfare. You are to "fight the good fight" (1 Timothy 6:12) and sometimes flee, shaking the dust off your feet. But these responses to evils must be taken up first into your more basic goal of following the way of Jesus. That way has love at its center: not revenge or earthly survival. The night before the crucifixion Peter tried to draw his sword to defend Jesus. Jesus said "no". Then Peter fled. John and Mary and Mary Magdalene and others chose neither fight nor flight but to stand under the cross.

Situations arise where you are brought to a standstill. You are at an impasse where the desire to fight or flee are in such conflict that you don't know which to choose. Do not act out of rage or fear. Cry out to Us so we can show you if there is another way that is better. Listen to the advice of holy friends. Then commend yourself to Us and act with confidence that We will bring good out of your decision.

July 23, 2008
Standing Your Ground Under the Cross

Holy Spirit: When in a conflict between two goods, you would like Our guidance to be a simple affirmation of your own greatest leaning. (I think the Holy Spirit wanted me to relate what follows to choices in my mind of fight or flight in a particular conflict situation.) Often you see the choice as between two extremes such as fight or flight. You add up the fantasized satisfactions of either course. You might not even think of trying instead for the cross of love and trusting that We will bring good out of the pain for all concerned. Jesus said "keep them in the world, but not of the world." (John 17:15) To be kept "in the world" is a counter to the desire to flee from conflict. To be kept from being "of the world" is a counter to fighting, as in pitting your natural strength against that of others. When you come to Us for guidance, then, try not to be self-protective but to be wide open for the way of love. In conflict, standing your ground under the cross might be avoiding hasty judgment in favor of deep listening.

July 24, 2008
"Everything Passes."

Holy Spirit: (This locution makes constant reference to the poem of St. Teresa: "May nothing disturb you. May nothing astonish you. Everything passes. God does not go away. Patience can attain anything. He who has God within, does not lack anything. God alone is sufficient.") You think you have let go of everything but "God alone," but at the threat of any change for the worst, you become frantic, "troubled and astonished," You want to cling to what you know. When it eludes your grasp, you have a choice: despair or trust. We allow that pain of real or seeming loss to help you to replace earthly possession with spiritual possession. "God is enough" because the source and depth of everything is in God.

Do you see how it is all in the Gospels? Mary Magdalene wants to hold onto the resurrected Christ, but he tells her "do not cling to me, I have not yet ascended to the Father." (John 20:17) He tells the disciples they cannot cling to Him, but He will not leave them orphans. They must be open to the Jesus they will find through Me, the Holy Spirit.

At the fear of loss, you beg Us for help. You may feel ashamed to be so needy; to want so desperately to possess. We tell you to look upward where your treasure is ascending. We promise that if you "seek first the kingdom of heaven, all things will be added unto you." (Matthew 6:33)

July 25, 2008
"Thy Will be Done!"

Holy Spirit: Your underlying motive for doing what is good can sometimes be to please others. Their pleasure in you makes you feel secure, that you won't lose them. It doesn't work. Why not? You are not a clone or a slave. There are limits on how well you can meet every need and desire of another human.

On the positive side, your own personhood seeks freedom to develop independently. Another person can reject you whenever you act not as a clone or as a slave. Then you feel devastated, cast out of relationship into a void. When you say the Lord's prayer: "Thy will be done," and mean it, you break through the dismal cycle of dependence on human affirmation. You seek a higher motive for your acts. Jesus certainly didn't please the powers of His time! In His human nature He had to be willing to accept the total rejection of most men to fulfill the will of His Father in heaven. It is because He knew Him so intimately as His Father that He could accept being crucified by men. Do you see how the phrase in the prayer "Thy will be done" comes as a result of the first line, "Our Father?" It is not a formula. It's a reality.

Through Sacraments and prayer, you become truly one with the Father. Then you have the strength to act out of the knowledge of being totally loved. More and more you are doing the will of the Father. You don't have to look around all the time to see if you are pleasing the people around you. The first step may be understanding this truth. That can happen in an instant. Only gradually, however, can We heal your hearts of the wounds of failed attempts at trying to find security in human love.

As this process continues, look at every choice you make and ask Us to help you answer questions such as these:

- Is this act good in itself?

- Am I doing it primarily because of its goodness (Thy will) or only to please a human? (How do you know? There are different ways, but one way to see is whether if human approval is lessened or removed, you still want to do it.) Then ask Us to give you wisdom and prudence and fortitude to carry out Our will. Accept that when you throw yourself whole-heartedly into what you think is God's will, you may be rejected or the work may be stopped by opponents or just circumstances.

(Today the conflict with the close friend was resolved with mutual forgiveness. Thanks be to Jesus, Mary, Joseph, God the Father, the Holy Spirit, and our angels. But I still felt kind of shattered and exhausted by it. This locution seemed as if the Holy Spirit was trying to bring truth out of it.)

July 26, 2008
Turbulence

Holy Spirit: It is hard for Us to keep you on the right path when you let your emotions run riot. You may enjoy emotional excitement, even when there is a lot of pain. It can seem preferable to the seeming monotony of quiet routines. The price of turbulence, though, is exhaustion, and often hurt feelings. We want, instead, to bring you into a state of vibrant receptivity. Open to Our presence. Let Us into the turmoil of your racing stream of thoughts and passions. In this way, We will be more and more a buffer zone between you and those around you. Instead of waiting to let Us in until you are desperate, let Us abide in you in a more constant way. Then, instead of nervous explosions, your words and actions will have the focus of love.

July 27, 2008
"Out of the Depths I Cry..." (Psalm 130:1)

Holy Spirit: A baby wails out of need for milk. There is a victory yell in sport. The lament for lost love is another kind of cry. There are cries of joy in song. The words of prayers you may mumble usually become a cry when your need is deep. Self-control is a virtue when it keeps you from trying to fulfill your passions through bad choices.

But self-control becomes distorted when it covers weakness by a show of invulnerability. The Devil wants you to suppress the cry from the depth. He wants you to see crying from the depth as weakness. He also wants you to cast aside discipline in letting wild passions free. Or, in fear of debilitating weakness, cry...."to You I lift up my soul." "Deep cries unto deep." (Psalm 42:7)

The way out of the impasse is up. We promise to assuage your deepest needs in ways you cannot foresee. In faith, cry out from the depth of your need.

July 28, 2008
Following Jesus

(This locution followed a conversation with someone involved in a religious community of women with different emphases than my Dedicated Widows of the Holy Family.)

Holy Spirit: You become perturbed when your ideas of how to follow Jesus clash with the ideas of others. You seek justification for your ideas through Scripture and Tradition. In this way, you try to make what is a way of life into something as absolute as dogma and doctrine. There is strength in common rules and practice, but what is maybe more needed in your times now is a way of the heart in response to the reality of Jesus. Your Jesus wants to permeate the world with faith, hope, and love.

Different types of community can grow around this experience. You can learn from what you try. Do you see the wisdom of the Church in looking not for rules and plans but rather for signs of good Christian living together in one form or another? Don't be afraid to make mistakes. When you encounter those with inspired plans, look not so much at the plan; that can be nothing but a fantasy. Look instead at the hearts of those involved and cherish the fruits of their works of love. Let Us show you what We want of you in relationship to the ways of life you encounter: Sometimes affirmation, sometimes that you are there to make suggestions; sometimes joining in. You cannot know which response is right in advance. Sense Our guidance in the encounter.

July 29, 2008
Freshness

Holy Spirit: Bombardments of the consequences of sin can make you feel trapped and constrained. Even when there is nothing immediately dangerous to you in your environment, there can be a staleness from repeated unwholesome patterns. Reach in and reach up to find cool freshness. "In" is the place within where We dwell, a pure stream of grace. "Up" is from your crouched position of fear to lift your arms and hands to greet the good, small and big, that We are sending you each day as fresh air.

Can you interrupt the stale round of your worries and unhealed memories to let in the new? Are you so afraid that if life isn't heaven it is really hell, that you are not savoring the foretastes of heaven, Our gifts for you each day?

July 30, 2008
"Finishing School"

Holy Spirit: In your culture in the past, awkward and sometimes wild girls used to be sent to a "finishing school" to be trained in proper deportment. They would graduate ready to come out in society as proper and elegant young ladies. By analogy, We try to train up immature and sometimes sinful followers to come out into the world as true soldiers of Christ. What We wish for, however, is not outward show but true conversion of heart from self-centered ways to the way of love. As your "final examination" in your "God Alone" training, we present you with this test: For a whole week, be so close to Us through prayer and intention so that your words and gestures will reflect love.

Don't be afraid this would destroy your free personality and make you a mere puppet. That is not what We want at all. No. If you give yourself to Us in this way, We will use all your natural gifts and God-created individuality in an even stronger way. Our grace will make a tentative melody into a symphony. Courage!

"Not I, but Christ lives in me."

July 31, 2008
More Love

Holy Spirit: There can never be too much love in the way you handle every encounter. We are helping you to make being loving your highest goal in your thoughts, words, and actions. Can you now see more clearly how specific this challenge is? How an unexpected sharp tone in your voice or in that of one who is speaking to you can hurt? How, on the other hand, a sudden strong expression of esteem or concern will melt a hardened heart? May this not be a passing phase but an earnest endeavor to which you are committed. Have you also begun to sense the greater attention to words of your liturgical prayers to change them from a good, dutiful chanting to a cry of love?

Of course, it is hard for you to understand the paradox of Our absolute Trinitarian transcendence and the need for love expressed, as has been discerned, in Jesus' cry: "I thirst," or in the commandment to love your God with your whole heart, mind, and strength. We help you with analogies: Is it weakness if parents cherish the love their children show them? Is it not rather bonding?

Don't be discouraged if your progress is slow. Learn from each setback. Remember, you are not alone. We are working in you.

August 1, 2008
Higher and Deeper

Holy Spirit: When We try to bring you up the mountain to a greater height, a wider view, you can feel overwhelmed. In one way, it is joy to be above the usual realm of earthly concerns. In another way, you can panic when you don't see the place for your feet to land. Suspension in the clouds is foreign to your bodily nature. An antidote to dizziness can be to feel your way deep into your roots. Your ultimate root, of course, is not a blood line only, but your source in the creating mind of the Father.

As a sign, I sometimes give the gift of tongues that you may speak an unknown language with primal sounds of roots deeper than our conscious mind. In some Hispanic paintings, God the Father in the image of an old regal man is depicted hovering behind Jesus, sustaining Him in an embrace, as Jesus is elevated on the Cross. Will you let the Father sustain you, also, from above and below?

"With groanings too deep for words." (Romans 8:23)

August 2, 2008
The Answer

Holy Spirit: You seek a single truth you could carry in to every circumstance of life. It would be like a password that opens every door. With this answer you would never again be perplexed and uncertain. It would end all doubt, shut the mouths of all scoffers. With this truth you could be strong instead of weak; luminous instead of murky – divine? A single word can sometimes be a lifeline, such as "light" or a battle cry such as "justice".

We see this longing for such a truth as your attempt to leap into eternity where "all will be one." You could also see this desire as a sign that you are coming closer to the kingdom of God where partial insights will merge into a unified vision. Each "answer" you find can be a path to God. It can take you so far, but not through the gate back to Paradise guarded by angels with flaming swords. (Genesis 3:24)

Sometimes you can only find the next path for your journey by becoming not more powerful to be able to destroy barriers, but smaller so you can sneak under them. Even as you are to avoid pride in your quest for the answer, it is better to push forward toward divine truth than to cling to inadequate formulas for coping in the world. Close your eyes and beg for the answer you need to take the next step forward.

(When I tried this what I got was something like "Openness; await the dawn vs. locked in by fear or closed into my own plans." It turned out I was on the verge of making a big move that would lead me to 8 years of teaching at Holy Apostles in Connecticut.)

August 3, 2008
Weakness

Holy Spirit: You honor weakness with your lips but not always with your heart. How is that? You understand from years of reading the New Testament that Jesus came to overcome the worldly sense of strength as coming from power. Instead He exalted the lowly, the meek. He responded with compassion and mercy to the humble and poor. On the other hand, in your own weakness, you want to lean on those who seem stronger than yourself'; stronger, for example, in intelligence or health, in accomplishments or in virtue. If you look at the saints, starting with Mary, what do you see? Not usually worldly strength but the power of love. As Christians you are to excel in compassionate love expressed in helping others in their needs. It is right to admire others for the strength of their virtues, and you can look up to them, but you need to lean more on the strength of God than on the strength of any human persons.

When you do this, you will be able to draw close to the weak that We send you. Instead of being afraid of their neediness you will be able to prudently give as we show you what will help them.

August 4, 2008
Leadership

(The context is that more widows are interested in my group, Dedicated Widows of the Holy Family, and I was having doubts I could lead them.)

Holy Spirit: You are afraid to lead because you think that followers will be as critical of you as you have been of past leaders you have followed. We want leaders who are well acquainted with their own flaws. Remember St. Peter so publicly weak in denying his Master? Do you see how his knowledge of his own betrayals made it possible to listen to Me in a dream about the food issues, or to Me through Paul about circumcision and the Gentile converts?

Beware of leaders who hate "suggestions boxes." If you are called into any leadership role, make yourself so humble and so eager to improve that the others will not be afraid to help you with suggestions. Disarm them with your humility. Always be eager to come to Us to listen. If your enterprises are a response to Our promptings, you will not need to think of yourself as defending your own ideas. Not that you should try to assume infallibility, claiming your decisions are influenced by Us. No! You can still make mistakes because the light of Our will is filtered through your dirty windows. We will use all your negative experiences of the past to help you avoid not only false moves but also false postures. When you think of leaders you have known in the past with clay feet, think not just of the clay but also of all the good for you We brought out of their initiatives.

August 5, 2008
Wordless Presence of God

Holy Spirit: Sometimes you can figure things out; sometimes you can't. You like to figure things out because you imagine that if you understand, you will be able to control things for the best. We like to see you exercise this God-given power of intellect. It is Our gift. How, then, can you accept it when you try to use the gift but no answer comes? That's when We want you to be like a child who can walk in the dark with a parent, hand in hand. Sometimes, like Peter, you swear your allegiance to follow Us even unto death, but when the test comes, your survival instinct pushes you to flee. We understand. We forgive. That you might be surer that you are forgiven, We give our priests the power to say the words of absolution for Us. After your words and deeds of penance, We want you to feel a wordless peace, like a child who was lost but then knows safety in the embrace of the parent.

August 6, 2008
Gusts of Grace

Holy Spirit: Just when you think that what you have done is enough, perhaps even more than enough, We send you a new gust of grace to do something more:

- to help a needy person;
- to start a new venture;
- to devise a new method of presentation.

At first you resist. Part of you wants not the new but rest from change. We understand. We don't prod you because your previous efforts are inadequate, but because the world is so hungry. Let Us work with you on these efforts so that your feeling is not pressure so much as wind in your sails.

"When I am weak, I am strong." (2 Corinthians 12:10)

August 7, 2008
Leadings

Holy Spirit: We want you to seek Our help and the help of your Mother, Mary, the angels and saints in your planning. That is good. You need guidance from on high. The saints always sought the virtue of prudence, enriched by other special gifts of discernment. Sometimes We make what We want very clear as when We told St. Joseph to flee from Herod with Mary and the child Jesus.

You want to feel that what you discern in prayer will give you certainty in the outcome of your decisions. This presents a problem. For instance, during the years that the holy family was in Egypt, Joseph had to trust without knowing how long it would be before Our plan would unfold for their return. When you feel insecure and anxious, you would like Us to reveal every detail of Our plan for you. Often We choose, instead, to show you only a step you can take next. (My godfather, Balduin Schwarz, used to tell me, "God's light is not a floodlight, but like the small ray of a flashlight on your path.") Future paths depend on free will responses of others. Some of these people you don't even know yet. Sometimes We want you to be part of a plan that fails on the surface because the failure will teach important lessons.

When you don't spend enough time in quiet prayer, your agitation prevents total reception of Our leads. You don't see, for instance, that your involvement in a plan may be not a change in location but rather encouragement of others, because there are things to do in your present place that have not yet shown themselves.

That is why in many circumstances, watchful waiting is better than leaping into something new. As We have been trying to teach you in many different ways, it is not good to become too attached to expectations, for often We work more through presences rather than visible direct outcomes. Look at the growth of the Church. Do you think the deaths of the martyrs seemed like success?

August 8, 2008
The Light of Truth

Holy Spirit: Our gifts to you include absolute truths shining in the darkness for all, and also words for the heart of each person. Some of you dislike the reality of universal truth which stands so strongly against the desire for individual autonomy. For example, a rebel rejects the "shalt" of the ten commandments: "Why not steal when I want something I can't otherwise have?" "Why should God be 3 persons instead of 4?" Others suspect, even more than universal truths, any personal truth given in prayer whether by directives or by signs. There is a correct wariness about being deceived by the devil or only one's own foolish wishes, such as wanting to sit at the right hand of God without first carrying the cross. But such wariness can close the doors to any heart-to-heart communication. Is the choice then between hard cold absolutes and sentimental fantasies?

"Blessed be the pure of heart for they shall see God." (Matthew 5:8) Jesus taught that deep truth comes to those with sincerity of purpose. The pure of heart treasure the light of truth revealed through writings or spoken teachings. They receive an individual word with "fear and trembling" and grateful humility: "Behold the handmaid of the Lord, be it done unto me according to Thy word."

To protect our children from the darkness of error, We provide the unchanging teachings of the Church and the guidance of the spiritually wise. When doubt and fear assail your poor little souls, hold fast to your Savior, the light shining in the darkness, who proclaims "the truth shall set you free." (John 8:32)

August 9, 2008
Envy

Holy Spirit: A toxic form of wounded pride is envy. It gnaws away at the fabric of family, the work place, and Church. Do you see how it dominates from the start? Satan envies God and influences Adam and Eve to wish to become godlike through rebellion. Cain envies Abel. Later, the brothers of Joseph sell him into slavery because of envy. Saul betrays David out of envy, all the way to most of the leaders in Jesus' time envying His authority and miracles. How much violence is rooted in envy! Watch closely for forms of envy in your dealings with others. The plain woman envies one more beautiful. The uneducated person envies the scholar. Others envy wealth and status. More subtle forms can be boasting, in the desire to provoke envy in others. Rage can come from impotent envy of those in power who ignore one's wishes or claims.

Each of you in your hearts must come to grips with your differences. You are to glimpse interiorly in prayer the providential love that is part of your circumstances. You have legitimate desires for bettering your life in small and big ways. If these spring from envy, it shows you are basically angry with God about your life. Instead, such desires for improving your lives should be a seeking for greater fullness. Such hopes are not for the downfall of others but for the same fullness in their lives.

There can be no place for envy if your motto is truly, "God Alone is Enough!"

Will you let Us show you that We are enough?

135

August 10, 2008
Shock Waves

Holy Spirit: Through advanced worldwide media coverage, you can be shocked not only by the evils in your immediate area, but those around the world. In a certain way, you have in your times more of a God's eye view of your world. In another way you are less aware. A family on a farm pre-media could watch things slowly grow. City people see these only as products in a supermarket. Through myriad events, personal and global, We immerse you in the rhythm of being of other creatures. At the same time, through the shock of destruction, small and large scale, you are weaned from making earth your home.

The tension of life, death, and new life reaches a climax in the events of the conception, birth, life, crucifixion, death, resurrection, and ascension of Jesus. You can participate in this cycle daily at the Mass, joining to it everything in your day of wonder, joy, shock, and transcendence. It all becomes too much for you. We let you sleep, and finally We lift you out and up. Meanwhile, soak it in!

August 11, 2008
Rising from the Ashes

Holy Spirit: The Church rose stronger from the era of the martyrs of pagan Roman massacres. Great grief overwhelms the faithful during the struggles throughout history. Think of the dark times of corruption within the Church in European history; of battles tearing apart countries and families. So, too, the martyrs of the 20th and 21st centuries and the scandals in the Church and the tearing apart coming from dissent. Do not succumb to violence of arms or rhetoric. Keep your eyes fixed on Jesus and let Him be the Savior, not only of your souls for heaven but also of your hope within the ashes of seeming defeat. Those of you whose lives have been relatively peaceful can be the most devastated when the bad times come.

Why? Why? Why? becomes your constant cry. Can you accept that help from Us comes not so much in outward change as deep change in your own hearts? Our saints. did they experience the triumph of their plans during their lives? Usually not! They had to plunge into the heart of God to get the strength to go on. Join with others not in rage but by clasping pierced hands.

136

"Be of good courage, for I have overcome the world." (John 16:33)

August 12, 2008
Saved

Holy Spirit: You would like your every enterprise to be successful with a minimum of labor and a maximum of profit. Sometimes that happens, but rarely. You would like Your spiritual life to be successful with a minimum of struggle and a maximum of applause. Sometimes that happens, but rarely. More often the success of an enterprise requires enormous effort for even a minimum of profit. More often holiness comes after terrible struggles with minutely-achieved visible change. What Jesus came to save was not your projects and products.

Neither did He die on the cross to save your "faces!" It is both simpler and more hidden. You are in anguish about your failures: less wealth instead of more; broken homes instead of family unity; war instead of peace; death instead of life. To be saved is not to be publicly crowned with success. It is to be forgiven and then given new life. New life is not for glory in human eyes but for mostly hidden gains, more kindness, more helpfulness, more sacrifice. And, hidden from public view is the permanent reward..."in the bosom of Abraham." (Luke 16:22-23)

August 13, 2008
God Within/God Above

Holy Spirit: Each era in Christian history has a different way of wrongly emphasizing more or less of the divinity or humanity of Christ. In your lifetime (1937 ff.), Catholics first thought of the divine nature of Christ as so transcending the human that they could scarcely dare to imagine Jesus performing ordinary physical human acts. By now, however, 2008, His humanity is so emphasized that some think of Him as being as weak as they are.

Phrases like "the God above" or "the God within" can usually seem neutral, but can take on the flavor of such divergences from the Truth. "God is above all thoughts" can become a way to keep Him away, so that your eyes are on the stars but your hearts are rooted in the world. "The God within" can become a way to keep Him imprisoned in your own categories, stripped of the power to change you.

Through Scripture and Tradition, We teach you balancing images.

Jesus offers parables of the Father's close love, such as the parable of the Prodigal son, but He also tells the disciples that "no one has seen the Father but Me." God is shown both as the farmer, sower of seeds, but then as the Judge separating the weeds from the grain. Let awe of the God above usher forth in praise while the heart opens to its all-consoling guest: the God within.

August 14, 2008
Family Stances

Holy Spirit: Each child in a family develops defenses against being taken over by the other children. The price of love can often be slavery to the other's wishes. Later, some become so defensive that they choose isolation rather than risk being used. Others attract companions, sometimes to replicate power positions of the past. How tragic! How bleak!

We want you to exit such a cycle. We want to help you do this. In the stories of the saints you see men and women who took in all the genuine love from their childhoods and the love that was there from others in their life as adults. They believed in the ideals of Christian love. Most of all, they opened their hearts to Our love: the Father, the Son, the Holy Spirit, and of Mother Mary, the angels and saints. They were liberated from patterns of power, defensiveness, and withdrawal. It is a never-ending battle between many-sided evils and victory through the power of love. Over and over in the Old Testament you see defeat if people trust in their own strength, and victory when they let themselves be the instruments of God's will.

In the Gospels, overturning the seemingly invincible plots coming out of fear, pride, jealousy and power, you see the triumph of divine love. You can try to analyze every aspect of psychological and spiritual warfare in life. That can only take you so far. Insight can lead to despair instead of breakthroughs.

Pray! Pray! Pray! Not to win others over to your side, but that fresh streams of divine love may bring change, forgiveness and change.

August 15, 2008
Holy Solitude

Holy Spirit: You crave company. Your often-lonely hearts cry out for human understanding and intimacy. Yet when human love is given, you can feel as if the price is too high. The others intrude into your inner space until you cannot even find yourself there. They can probe your motives until you cannot even find any pure reasons for doing anything. Can you see that many in these times are choosing a more solitary life? Is this because they are failures in relationships? Sometimes. But also, for some, because We are drawing them out from the crowd.

Sometimes the greater isolation is physical; sometimes it is mental. Sometimes it is purely spiritual – as in going within to Us in the midst of people. To feel it unbearable to be alone is to deny Our presence with you. Our presence is mysterious: potentially burning, but oftentimes almost cool. Our demands are sometimes for change in your decisions, but often just that you be free enough to be present to Us. The words of worship and other formal prayers will draw you out and up to Us. Please don't resist.

"And we shall come make our dwelling in them."

August 16, 2008
Talents

Holy Spirit: Many times, you have to do things in life with painful difficulty against the grain. We grace your efforts. Other times, what you are called to do for love of Us and for love of your brothers and sisters flows easily from the talents We have given you in abundance. The Evil one, knowing the power of those talents, tries first to bend them to bad purposes: unusual intelligence can be bent to bad aims; unusual intelligence can be bent toward conquest; unusual strength toward brutality; unusual physical beauty toward seduction.

When the talents are directed by love, the Evil One works more subtly. Into dedication he mixes pride. Into commitment he mixes neglect of other claims. Perseverance can be pushed to exhaustion. Watch out for the self-doubt that surfaces when you sense the mixture of these negatives with your talents. The doubt leads to a desire to give up. Instead of giving up, you need to bring your talents back to Us, their source, for purification and renewal. Then they will shine for whoever we have prepared them to reach.

"My soul magnifies the Lord and my spirit rejoices in God my Savior." (Luke 1:46-47)

August 17, 2008

"A Prophet is not Honored in His own Country." (Matthew 13:57)

Holy Spirit: In the sentimental religion of your fantasies, sincerity is always rewarded with applause. In the sentimental scenario of your fantasies, to be right is always to be victorious. In the sentimental world of your fantasies, your own family is the first to accept your prophetic charism.

Examine the life of your model Jesus, and the history of the Church. Do you hear Applause? What do you see? Victory? What do the records show? Families affirming the path of the countercultural path of the martyrs? The history is full of paradox: the "prince of peace" carries a 2-edged sword. (Hebrews 4:12.) At some periods, saints followed the claims of opposed leaders. When you are nailed to the cross by rejection, some of you want to flee; others want to scream denunciations. While you await Our next move, take up the words of your model: "Father, forgive them, they know not what they do." (Luke 23:34)

August 18, 2008
Tug of War

Holy Spirit: Each one pulls hard. To win is to overcome the resistance of the opponent. Once toppled and fallen, the "enemy" can be dragged to the side of the victor. This game is played over and over again in daily power struggles. Sometimes the outcome is predictable. A parent has the strength to compel the disobedient child to comply. The more skilled competitor in a sport will outrace the ones less able.

What is it in humans that revels in such trials of strength? Is it a matter of natural delight in power, or is it ugly and evil pride? Of course, it can be either. Looking at the negative type of tug of war, can some only enjoy superiority by forcing another into submission? For believers, tugs of war become more complex trials. Love of power is to be conquered by the power of love. In the process there is no lack of bloodshed. You cannot figure it all out beforehand. At any moment, self-assertion can overtake the goal of love. Consider the familiar display: three men on crosses. Each one has lost the tug of war with the Roman conquerors. In defeat, the bad thief tries for a last power play by taunting Jesus as a false Messiah.

Your Savior takes a different path. He speaks out of the despair of seeming defeat: "My God, My God, why have you forsaken Me?" (Matthew 27:46) Then he changes the nature of the trial in the words, "Into Your hands I commend My spirit." Jesus lifts the battle from the physical realm. He shows you that what really counts is the battle to keep faith in the Father's love in spite of all appearances. Out of the victory of hope over despair, He has an overflow of mercy to forgive His earthly enemies, "Father, forgive them, they know not what they do." (Luke 23:34)

As if sensing the shift to the new battleground, the good thief begs Jesus for a secret supernatural victory even for himself, a man justly condemned to death. When you find yourself losing the tug of war in your attempts to get what you want, which of the three on the cross will you imitate: the bad thief taunting God for not helping him win; Jesus, trusting the Father to bring a higher victory; or, like the good thief, putting all your hope on the Redeemer? Sometimes it is good for men to cry and to cry out. (A few minutes after this locution, I thought the Holy Spirit added: Do you see how the Mercy Chaplet shifts you from love of power to the power of love?)

August 19, 2008
Hardness

Holy Spirit: Our St. Augustine thought that "peace is the tranquility of order." You can love order as a relief from chaos. Order is good. Sometimes, though, the desire for order can make you tense and hard. You see that your goals are blocked by others because they are more relaxed or just indifferent, or busy with other goals. You seek their cooperation. You can try persuasion or you can try force. In either attempt, persuasion or force, beware of becoming hard. Hardness manifests the fact that the goal of order is higher to you than the goal of love. Even though the goal of order is loving, you are letting the ends justify the means when your approach is hard. As you go about your daily rounds, even when you are alone, check from time to time for tension and hardness. When you detect either of them, stop, even for a minute. Lift your heart to Us for a fresh flow of lighter energy. Avoid efficiency at any price.

"What does it profit a man to gain the whole world and lose his immortal soul?" (Luke 9:25)

August 20, 2008
Persecution

Holy Spirit: In the academic world, you think of positions taken on one side or another of a debate as if the point of view was the important thing, not the persons holding them. In seeking truth, this can be a good way to think. In the world outside the school, however, differences soon become highly personal as the consequences of ideas mount up. Those whose ideas are threatened by greater numbers on the other side will sometimes resort to violent retaliation. Think of the leaders who felt threatened by the growing popularity of Jesus and reacted by persecuting Him unto death. On the verbal level, when you feel you cannot win over the opposition, you may resort to the "violence" of sarcasm or name-calling. If the debate is between people who know each other well, the feeling of being persecuted is especially wounding. How are you, a follower of Jesus, to conduct yourself under verbal attack? Jesus was not naïve about the motives of those who were against Him. Neither should you be. Yet He accepted seeming defeat in the events leading to His passion and death. He who had the divine power to destroy His enemies, instead chose the way of silence and even of forgiveness. Should you do less?

August 21, 2008
Judas and Mary

Holy Spirit: Judas saw no way out. He tried to find it by destroying himself. You read about him and you wish he had waited for the resurrection and then begged Jesus for forgiveness. When Mary saw no way out, no way to protect her son from violence and death, she stood under the cross, her soul given over to anguish, but also to seemingly futile acts of heroic hope and trust.

Many times, the children of God are nailed to the cross. They beg to be taken down from the cross, or at least to know why. When you are nailed to the cross, it is not wrong like Jesus to cry out, "Why have you forsaken me?" but you need also over and over again in your trials to pray like Jesus, "Into your hands I commend my spirit." The Passion tells you that what counts is not to escape from suffering, but to endure it with trust in the Father's plan and then let him liberate you as He chooses, for even if your enemies kill you, you will be saved in heaven. Do you see that in some situations there is no solution in

142

earthly terms, and your only choice is between stark despair and stark hope in God Alone?

"Holy Mary, Mother of God, pray for us sinners now and at the hour of our death."

August 22, 2008
Unity of Purpose

Holy Spirit: Your strength is broken when there are major divisions in your efforts. In the Bible, you see this beginning with Satan falling from heaven, and Adam and Eve falling away from unity with God, and Cain and Abel at enmity. In reverse, you see strength when there is unity of purpose: Joseph, when in power, helping his brothers; David defending Saul; Peter and Paul coming to agreement. Can you see how weakened is the Christian witness by divisions between groups and within groups? Unity can be based on warding off enemies. The Zealots of Jesus' time on earth were united in purpose trying to overthrow the Roman dominance. In your present world, there can be political strength when forces unite to repel an enemy.

More important, however, is that you have a common positive purpose that We call the building of the kingdom of God. Think of the strength of beauty when voices join together in song, when members of families set aside individual goals for a common effort. To be strong for the kingdom of God, you need Our gifts of faith, hope, and charity. These overcome the division that comes with doubt, despair, and rejection. When you come to prayer, you open to these gifts, and then by your unity of purpose with Us you are strengthened to bring faith, hope, and love to others.

Do you see how doubt, despair, and anger are quicksand for the kingdom of God? Never let them grow in your heart. Cast yourself into Our unity so we can show you how to bring the most light, peace, and love into each situation you encounter. If you cannot win a victory over evil on earth, let us help you win the battle within your own heart.

Pray, pray, pray.

"God Alone is Enough."

[If you got a lot out of reading *God Alone is Enough* and want to give it to someone else, separate from this whole book, *Further*

*Along...*you can obtain it for free by googling *God Alone* by Ronda Chervin.]

(After the final locution in the above series, it seemed as if the Holy Spirit wanted to stop this sequence of some 85 little "essays" and instead give me personal advice about each day's concerns. After a long, long, hiatus, in the year 2014 these messages or words of the heart, or locutions came again. I put them under the title of *Healing of My Heart.* These are now included in *6 Toes in Eternity*, available at En Route Books and Media – just google the title with my name, and the link to *6 Toes* will come up.

Last Teaching Position

When I was living near my daughter Carla's house in North Carolina, a widow looking into becoming a dedicated widow in community told me about a priest in Connecticut who was forming a community that would include priests, Sisters, married Catholics, singles, and widows. Always seeking utopian communities, I visited the priest, and finding him to be magisterial, charismatic, and with a heart for the poor, I decided to move there to try it out.

Guess what? I didn't fit in as much as I thought I would.

As I write these words, I am thinking that it is natural to long for perfect places to live since we are destined for a perfect place, called heaven. But it is almost a slur on that gift to try to conceive of finding that on earth. What makes heaven perfect is the full presence of God. No humanly-devised place can give us that happiness. There is nothing wrong with considering possibilities. Widows want the shelter of a place to be with others of the kingdom, to share hope. What is bad about the way I do it is the desperation. Peace is a gift from the Father, not a result of perfect planning. When I feel that rising of bubbly joy, I need to gently place myself into the arms of the Holy Family and ask that they give me the grace to accept whatever plan for the rest of my life God the Father has in mind for me.

However, in the process of discerning that community, I discovered that there was a seminary right nearby that needed a philosophy professor. So, in 2009, I agreed to barter teaching for room and board. This teaching position at Holy Apostles College and Seminary lasted 7 years, the longest amount of time I spent anywhere after my husband's death. During that time, I wrote some new books including *Last Call: 12 Men who Dared Answer* (about late vocations), *Spirituality for Our Times* (co-author Kathleen Brouillette), and *Way of Love*.

I was brought into this institution's online learning program. Students were from all over the world, including Eritrea, using their computers. When Dr. Sebastian Mahfood became the administrator of this program, we team-taught a course on Atheism, leading to the book *Catholic Realism: How to Refute Atheism and Evangelize Atheists*.

With the help of Bob Olson, a wonderful lay evangelist who had been a radio sportscaster, Sebastian started a Catholic radio station (WCAT Radio). He and I also started a Catholic press, En Route Books and Media. A program called *Why I am Still a Catholic,* that I facilitated, led to a series of booklets with that title published by goodbooksmedia .com. The radio shows are now a book called *Short Takes...*

Friends, Marti Armstrong and Dale Noble

You might also like to check out sometimes the numerous YouTube channels that have been made of talks through the years. "Ronda Chervin YouTube" searching does the trick. By the way, I never knew about most of these. Techie people put them up as they wish.

In many ways, my time at Holy Apostles was a culmination of my vocation in teaching. Having a Rector, Fr. Douglas Mosey, who was such a great priest and adminis-trator was a fantastic boon! The classes were attended by seminari-ans, by lay students, and by a large contingent of Vietnamese Sisters and Seminarians. Every morning, I was at Holy Masses with beautiful choirs and inspiring homilies. I received spiritual direction from a priest professor and then from a parish priest. Three times a day I was at table in the cafeteria talking to ardent Catholics... a prayer group with Carol Gignac. It was here that I met Marti Arm-strong, who became a Dedicated Widow and one of the closest friends of my whole life.

My circle of friends came to include a volunteer tutor at Holy Apostles, Dale Noble, who assisted me with rides and tech and prudent advice. Dale and I have a friendship of opposites. Where I am tense and workaholic, Dale is relaxed and laid-back. Not that she doesn't do a lot for others, but never in an uptight

Dale Noble.

manner. Where I am overly idealistic, Dale is a super-savvy woman who knows the real score. God bless you, Dale.

During my years at Holy Apostles, I also gave workshops to Catholics from nearby parishes. One of the participants, pro-life activist and poet, David Dowd, remained a friend after I left.

Louise and I at church.

Some women such as Louise Walkup who had been reading my books for decades met me for the first time. Louise, Dave Basconi, Maria Smith, Brenda Peters, and others eventually became a panel on a radio show on WCAT called RondaView. Check it out!

During my time in Connecticut God sent me a friend who has become closer and closer through the years: Jacke Brinker. She is an artist whose work I think should be in galleries. I have included here a photo of her and my favorite painting of hers.

At one point, having difficulty with the cold on the East Coast, I decided to take a 6-months' leave of absence and live with my daughter, Diana, in Orange County, California. It was wonderful to be with this family, especially my daughter, who is full of joy and love and is also an artist and craftsperson.

I loved being part of the Legion of Mary chapter in the nearby parish. In my utopian dream, I would go door-to-door, and all these lapsed Catholics or non-Catholics would stream back to our Church! In actuality, the members of the group eventually told me very gently that my tendency to argue with the people I met was not Legion pol-

Jacke Brinker.

Jacke's painting.

icy. I did much better as a Legion of Mary member, going around to shut-ins with Holy Communion!

Back to Holy Apostles, how did I do on Drama Queen and Utopianism? Sadly, still not so good. The drama queen bit came out especially in the dining room. I would love to regale people with anecdotes from my colorful past. And, worse, I would get into long arguments about controversial Church subjects such as charismatic gifts and the alleged visions at Medjugorje, booming out my point of view in a loud voice.

How is this for a check-mate on drama queen:

Priest: How about counting up the number of times your sentences begin with "I"?

Ronda: But otherwise people at the table only do small-talk or even remain silent!

Priest: Well I think that when you call yourself an egocentric maniac, it is not a joke. You are!

Ronda: So, if think these horrible things about me, why do you want to be my friend?

Priest: Well, you have some good points.

After some tears, I went to confession to a different priest. A seminarian friend told me that when he overheard such arguments, he could almost see Jesus walking away!

Of course, with my fear of rejection complex, I assumed the priest who delivered the insults would never talk to me again. How healing it was that he remained my friend and gave me good advice about other subjects. A one-liner from him that I cherish is this: "Don't think less of yourself; think of yourself less!"

Utopian problems? Well, Holy Apostles was one of the best places I had ever been. Just the same, the utopia syndrome came out when I was working on a complicated writing project. In this Church, we professors often referred to what was called jocularly, "the *de facto* schism"! So much division about issues involving sexual morality, social justice, roles of women and men, war and peace, etc.

In a manic utopian mood, I devised the idea of a course based on an anthology of articles I would assemble which would be called *Toward a 21st Century World View: Healing Divisions in the Church.* The chapters would be written by professors and grad students in the on-campus and online programs of Holy Apostles. The articles were full of important truths and were beautifully illustrated by Jim Ridley of Goodbooksmedia, the publisher.

Just the same, when I began teaching the book with as many of the authors as possible coming in to talk about their subjects, divisions augmented at our campus itself! Key dramatic "every utopia becomes a gulag" moments were these: The professor who wrote the article about liturgy was deeply into justifications for the revival of the Latin Extraordinary Form of the Mass. I remember when I first became a Catholic and the first Masses in English came along, I remarked prophetically, "Someday the Latin Mass will come back as an exotic innovation."

So, sitting around the seminar table in the class, a student who loved praise-filled Hispanic Masses began to argue with the professor who wrote the article that before such Masses, he found the Mass boring!

You probably can write the rest of the discussion!

In another instance, a grad student who was part of the Peace Movement was summarizing his chapter about pacifism. A Vietnamese seminarian whose father and uncle had been generals in the Vietnamese War related this story: "My uncle captured a village in South Vietnam that had been taken over by the North Vietnamese Communists. Because he was a Catholic, he treated the enemy charitably. But then later on, he was captured by the Communists. They cut off his arms and legs." Silence filled the room.

Such conflicts in a classroom are nothing compared to real gulags. But they served to puncture my utopian idea that I could fix divisions in the Church with a beautifully written overarching textbook!

I would be remiss if I didn't mention the usual reason I had for going to the Sacrament of Reconciliation. You may be surprised to know that in most seminaries, confession is available every day of the week! We think this is because evil spirits are especially keen on defeating future priests.

So what was my most popular sin? Rage at tech! Having studied typing as a teenager, when computers came in, I thought I would be good at it. Not at all. Because I was a writer, I had to either adjust to computers for writing my manuscripts or give up being a writer. No contemporary publishers want hefty hard copies of an author's writings.

Much easier than sending back manuscripts with rejection slips is a quick form email politely saying, "Your project, unfortunately, doesn't fit into our line." Since I truly am slightly disabled in the area of hand-eye coordination, the multitudinous new-fangled devices of tech are so difficult that I find myself yelling at my PC in frustration. My confessors try to hide their smiles at my drama-queen descriptions of my venial sins of anger at tech.

This chapter has been very short. Because of all my good memories of this wonderful institution, Holy Apostles College and Seminary, I thought it deserved its own chapter. However, the Holy Spirit seemed to advise me to avoid any longer descriptions and go on quickly to the last phase of my life.

Retired Great-Grandmother

"In old age, still full of sap, still green." (Psalm 92:14)
"Be not afraid." (Matthew 28:10)
"Remain at peace and attend to your own affairs." (1 Thess. 4:10)

Way before retiring, I had done a lot of thinking about retirement. One of the books I wrote that I like the best and that I used in parish ministry is *Seeking Christ in the Joys and Sufferings of Aging*. (Presently distributed by En Route Books)

I wrote this book when I was 58 and heading for the 60 crisis I anticipated. Here are some of the features of my book that readers got a lot out of:

Long lists compiled from workshop participants' sharings about joys and sufferings of aging. My all-time favorites on joys were, "since I turned 70, when it rains, I let it," and, "As an old woman, I can poke anyone any time and they don't mind!"

Excellent advice from a psychologist about how retired people need balance, as in we need some activities without too much pressure, but with ample contemplative-style leisure.

Proofs for the immortality of the soul, scriptures about death and resurrection, and inspiring anecdotes about the deathbeds of saints.

In another, quite different endeavor, I assembled anthologies of memoirs of older members of groups I ran for writers. One of these books is called *Fabric of our Lives*. The writers told stories of how a particular piece of cloth symbolized a key episode in their lives: as in the bathrobe of her father who died, handed down to the writer who wears it now herself for comfort. *Legacy: How to Write your Memories for Family and Friends* provides sample stories from my writers with space for the reader to insert his or her own. My first Holy Communion, My First Kiss, Trips, Surviving the Worst, etc.

Of much greater weight was a book I co-authored called *What the Saints Said about Heaven* with theologians Richard and Ruth Ballard. Published by Tan/St. Benedict's, it includes the truths of the faith explained by Richard, icons by artist/theologian Ruth, and prayerful meditations by me.

A small, small, book I wrote long, long, ago *is Victory Over Death* – a book designed for anyone haunted by doubts about the reality of life after death.

You would think all of this research and pondering would totally prepare me for retirement. Not really! I once heard about Sister teachers in a convalescent home of their order who spent lots of time every day putting on blackboards the multiplication table!

Here is a photo of myself with Francette and Yvonne, good Corpus Christi friends.

Think about it. Teachers are used to being the center of attention; of having the power to command obedience; and being the "oracle" of truth. Now in how many situations, in which an 80-year-old retired teacher finds herself, can any of these usual perks prevail?

All right already, Ronda, tell us your retirement story.

In the year 2016, I retired from Seminary teaching and went to live in Corpus Christi, Texas.

Escape from 20 degrees below in the winter in Connecticut!

Escape from the pressure of grading and meetings!

I decided to go to Corpus Christi, Texas because of good memories of the balmy heat, good friends from teaching there in the past, and closeness of my blog-master and publisher Jim Ridley and other dear friends.

Jesus once allegedly told me: We like to surprise you.

The big surprise in Corpus Christi was the friendship and spiritual direction of Al Hughes, with whom I wrote 3 books in a year and a half.

Al Hughes, a former Lieutenant Colonel in the Air Force, was a convert from atheism, a retired former Dean of the college I worked at many years ago, a spiritual director, and now a retired widower. When together at the same college here in Corpus Christi, I had persuaded him to join my group for writers. The result was an autobiographical book called *Paradise Commander* published by our mutual friend, Jim Ridley of goodbooksmedia, and some other books, too. Having lots of time on his hands, he offered to take me from the apartment I was living in to Masses at his favorite Church: Our Lady of Guadalupe with a dynamic, magisterial priest, Fr. James Farfaglia. It is a Hispanic parish with a big outreach to youth who might otherwise be swallowed up in gang-life.

I had a bright idea! Why not write together a novel describing a utopian Catholic community for retired people! If we made it attractive enough, perhaps I could persuade my dear old friend, Francette Meaney, who owned lots of property to build it for us, our friends, and herself should she someday become a widow.

Well, without using the phrase "Every Utopia becomes a Gulag," Al Hughes, a practical former Air Force Colonel, gently suggested that meeting at Holy Mass, having a dinner together now and then, and gathering a group for writers would be

Al Hughes and I.

much more feasible! Simultaneously, Al with his spiritual director's eye, noticed that I was always picking nervously at my fingernails. A symptom of anxiety? Since I was looking for a spiritual director in my new retirement area, I quickly persuaded him to play that role.

Now, look how God brings good out of evil! A few weeks into our sessions I think: "Gee, Al's ideas are very good. Why don't we write a book together that is a chronicle of my reported woes of anxiety and Al's insights? It would be a sort of new genre, since nobody I ever heard of was so open and transparent as to put into print the details of the miseries she or he confided to a spiritual director with his concrete advice. A year later: *Escaping Anxiety on the Road to Spiritual Joy*, my last major book. Here is a photo of us from the back cover of that book:

Then came another co-authored book with Al Hughes: *Simple Holiness*...and finally one called *Road-Map For 80-year-olds*. These were all gobbled up by dear Sebastian Mahfood for En Route Books.

The insights in *Escaping Anxiety*... that I have found most helpful for me and others are these. First of all, Al helped me identify what he calls the "bitter root judgment" underlying anxiety. In his own case, it

153

was thinking he was ugly because of his father's lack of affection and being bullied at school. In my case, it was fear of rejection, especially by men, because of my father's leaving our family when we twins were 8 years old. The key spiritual practice for healing of anxiety, according to Al Hughes, is to pray with enough depth so that I will know the personal love of Jesus for me enough to accept whatever His permissive will allows. It is impossible to quickly summarize the whole book, so if you are a reader with anxiety problems, or know others who are, google *Escaping Anxiety on the Road to Spiritual Joy*.

I loved the beautiful bay of Corpus Christi. I loved the warm weather. I loved my friends. I loved the parish I was in where I volunteered.

So, why didn't I stay? It's simple: at 81 years old I didn't want to live alone. I joke about dementia, but even though I don't have it according to a test a doctor did, I still have senior moments at a higher rate each week! Here is what lured me away. A granddaughter of mine, Jenny Hurt, a revert Catholic, married to a convert from an atheist background, now daily Mass Catholics with a little child and a baby, invited me to live with them in Hot Springs, Arkansas. I would contribute most of my social security and pension in exchange for living in their rented home, dinner with them each evening, family rosary, and a promised daily ride to Mass. Dr. Sean Hurt, my grandson-in-law, is a professor of geology at National Park College here.

When this was in the planning stage, I called up one of the two parishes in Hot Springs. Without giving my name, I said: "I am moving to Hot Springs and I am a strong Catholic. Can you tell me if your Church is progressive, moderate, or strongly with Church teaching?" The receptionist yelled into the phone, "We are magisterial because our Bishop is!"

Great Granddaughters:
Teresa and Julia

Jenny and Sean.

Four generations. Diana, daughter on top, Jenny, granddaughter, me and little Teresa first great granddaughter.

We have not felt let down at this Church. And we are renting a huge house with an in-law suite, right on the lake.

Has Ronda, drama queen, found utopia at last?

Well, believe it or not, I really enjoy gazing at the lake, at birds and squirrels, especially at my great grand-children, and even helping with dishes and laundry. I think that retired 80-year-olds want to do easy things. What is much easier than I thought was living with Jenny and Sean Hurt and the great grandchildren: Teresa (4 years old) and Julia (8 months old at the time of writing this chapter).

[insert the two Hurt family photos, need captions]

I was sure I would love being with fervent daily Mass Catholics. I do. What I didn't reckon on is how Jenny and Sean have virtues that work to block my drama queen and utopian tendencies! Which virtues? How about both being relaxed vs. always tense like me! How about being prudent vs. spacey like me! How about being patient vs. needing to have closure yesterday if possible like me!

Grandson Nicholas with his wife, Veronica

Grandson Alex with his wife, Ioana

Grandson Max with his girlfriend, Aliza

Bonus virtues:

How about Sean being a gourmet cook vs. eating mostly left-overs in soups like me!

How about Jenny being physically beautiful in her youth vs. skeletal and wrinkled like me!

Now, if I let them add to this chapter, I am sure they would have good to say about me, but they can save all that for the eulogy they will deliver on the day my nine toes leap into Eternity.

A new joy is the friendship of the wives of 2 of my adult grandsons and the steady girlfriend of another. See how wonderful they are.

And, in spite of my hatred of tech, I have to praise God for video chats where I can see all my family members live.

But so many little things are hard to do at my age – like even opening jars! I humorously challenge myself this way: If someone gave me $500 to do this, would I figure out a way? Yes!

So, have I become a saint?

Not really! Sad to say, I am not yet a saint. Dietrich Von Hildebrand used to say, "there is an abyss between an ardent Catholic and a saint," and I am at the lower end of the abyss despite all the graces God has poured into my little soul all these years!

Am I in despair? No! My little joke is that God can't send me to hell because I try so hard. God has got to put me in Purgatory, if only for effort! And then one day, heaven, the true Utopia, where better than being drama queen is being in eternal bliss with God in the kingdom for an infinity of time.

I like to joke about my funeral one day. I say, I will have a tape of my voice tucked away in the coffin. After the Mass for the Dead, the priest will push a button, and the mourners will hear this: "You knew I would get the last word, didn't you? Now, my only message to my son-in-laws is this. Please forgive me for whatever annoyed you about me the most. You can save telling what it was for the reception. If any of you dear family and friends want to see me again but you are not practicing Catholics, there are a few priests here at the funeral. Go to Confession, and come back to the sacraments! Or, if you are not yet Catholics, sign up for classes!

Since so far, I haven't found a priest willing to execute this Last Will and Testament, I decided instead to put together a little book called

9 Toes in Eternity. My friend and publisher, Jim Ridley, of goodbooks-media put in this subtitle, "A sagacious salmagundi of one-liners, sacro-saws, holy quips and pious quotes composed or compiled by Ronda Chervin for distribution at her funeral!

Here are a few excerpts to attract you:

(Jesus asked): "Why would you want to do anything without Me?"

"Don't dog-paddle in the waves of life, but let me, Jesus, float you to the shore."

(Speaking to my cat, Cleo): "Ah, Cleo, some of us wonder how Jesus can stand us, since there is an abyss between his Divinity and our smallness, but there is an abyss between a human and a cat, yet I have no trouble loving you and, even if you sometimes bite and scratch, I try to tame you, but I don't reject you!"

"You who fear rejection:

    not by grabbing

    trying to capture

    locking the door...

Come inside My Heart"

    where I make all to be one."

"Stop scheming to avoid suffering."

"Go slowly (lento), not jerkily (staccato), through each day."

"In your last decades, think of yourself less as a captain and more like a lighthouse."

"When you feel afraid, take My pierced hand and let Me lead you up the mountain of life to heaven.

(About Daily Mass for retired people who can easily come): "If Jesus wants to leap from heaven into my body, shouldn't I be there to receive Him?"

I end the booklet with the lines of a favorite Gospel song:

"If I get to heaven before you do, I'll dig a little hole and pull you through!"

The end of this account of my life must include one of the saddest parts: the death from a blood clot of my daughter, Carla, after years of lymphoma from which she seemed to have been healed. It is too painful to recount this part of my life...except to say that in the end she got her wish was that she would receive the anointing of the sick and a Catholic funeral in spite of being most of her life outside the sacraments. If you wish to know more about this, e-mail me at chervinronda@gmail.com and I will send you my account.

Living with the Hurts, my wonderful Catholic home-schoolers, didn't work out...I am now looking into other possibilities.

Let me close *Further Along the Road* with some of my favorite Scriptures at this time:

"Be still and know that I am God." (Psalm 46:10)

"May Christ dwell in your hearts through faith, and may charity be the root and foundation of your life. Thus you will be able to grasp fully, with all the holy ones, the breadth and length and height and depth of Christ's love, and experience this love which surpasses all knowledge, so that you may attain to the fullness of God himself." (Ephesians 3:18)

"That your joy may be full." (John 15:11)

Prayer for Widows

GOD THE FATHER,
I offer you the rest of my time on earth
that I may serve with love and come to eternal life.
May my husband be blessed on his journey in eternity
and everyone in my family be saved.

Holy Spirit, be a comfort to all widows, especially the newly be-
reaved. Jesus, my bridegroom, savior of my soul, delight of my heart,
help me. Mary, exalted widow, mother of the Church, my model and
intercessor; pray for me.
St. Joseph, protector of Mary and the child Jesus,
and helper of widows,
guide me in the trials of daily life. St. John,
helper of the widow Mary, pray for me.
As a widow, may I be a spiritual mother to all I meet today.

(note: some widows like the first half of this prayer above, but can't
pronounce parts of the names in the second part, so just pray the first
part).

All you widow saints, pray for me:

St. Monica, pray for me
St. Paula, pray for me
St. Elizabeth of Hungary, pray for me
Blessed Angela of Foligno, pray for me
St. Elizabeth of Portugal, pray for me
St. Bridget of Sweden, pray for me
St. Rita of Cascia, pray for me
St. Frances of Rome, pray for me
St. Catherine of Genoa, pray for me

St. Jane of Chantal, pray for me
Blessed Marie of the Incarnation, pray for me
St. Louise de Marillac, pray for me
Blessed Marguerite d'Youville, pray for me
St. Elizabeth Seton, pray for me
Servant of God Praxedes Fernandez, pray for me.
Ven. Conchita of Mexico, pray for me.
All other widows now in heaven,
pray for me.

Stations of the Cross for Widows

(from *Walk with Me, Jesus: A Widow's Journey.*
Simon Peter Press, 2008)

The First Station: Jesus is Condemned to Death

Mary...

Your Son, who was to be judge of all the living and the dead, stood before a Roman judge and received an unjust sentence. Though you knew He was the "suffering servant" prophesied by Isaiah, did you wonder why He had to suffer this humiliation and in this way?

As widows, we sometimes question God's providence – and His love for us.

- Why did that drunk driver who killed my husband survive?
- Why did God permit that doctor's mistake?
- Was there anything done – or left undone – that hastened the day or the hour?
- Why did my husband have to die instead of me?

Holy Mary, pray for us ... now and in the hour we cry for justice.

Jesus: You are the Lord of my life. I know that You permit only those things from which You can bring good. Help me to trust that even the day and the hour of my husband's death was known to You, and that he is enfolded in Your Sacred Heart now as then.

The Second Station: Jesus Accepts the Cross

Mary ...

Many of us spent long hours at the bedside of our husbands, anticipating the separation that would come. Others of us experienced the tragedy of our spouse's sudden, unexpected death.

Just as nothing you could have said would have persuaded Jesus to evade the cross, we had no choice but to accept what we could not change.

The heaviness of that cross drained us, even as we persevered in hope.

Holy Mary, pray for us, that with each passing day this temporary separation will lead to everlasting joy.

Jesus, You endured all the trials we face, up to and including that final, wooden cross. You are with us every moment in the pain, and up to those final moments of our husband's earthly life. Then and now, You want us to rest our weary heads in Your lap so that you can console us ... but we are too busy coping to come to You. As we look upon the second station and see You accepting Your cross, let us also see that You were holding us up through the intensity of our pain and loss.

Third Station: Jesus Falls for the First Time

Mary ...

You saw your strong, manly son fall under the terrific weight of those beams. As you watched helplessly, waves of weakness filled your own body.

Did those feelings remind you of the grief you felt when Joseph died?

Watch over us, as our own physical strength dwindles slowly. Stay with us after the funeral, when we can hardly rise from our beds.

We, too, have felt those times of weakness that threatened to overtake us. Sometimes they linger still. Watch over us and lend us your strength and help us to move forward in hope.

Jesus, when widows collapse under the strain of early widowhood, You never chide us for failing to take up daily life tasks with our usual efficiency. Instead, You remain at our side each day, and hover over our solitary beds, sending invisible graces. May we never doubt Your love for us as You bring new strength to our new state of life.

Fourth Station: Jesus Meets His Mother

Mary ...

As I meditate upon this station of the Cross, I am struck by what an unforgettable encounter this must have been between you and your Son. It reminds us that deeper even than shared joy is shared agony!

Pray for us now. Some of us looked into the eyes of our husbands as they left this world. Some had no chance to say goodbye – he died far away or instantaneously, without warning.

Pray for us, your abandoned daughters.

Jesus, You knew Your mother's heart inside out. Though it comforted You to receive her last touch and glance, it also must have grieved You to be the cause of her pain. Thank you for the family and friends, priests, and parishioners who stayed with us as we made our way of the cross with our husbands. Even if no one walked with us, You, Jesus, Your mother, our angels and the widow saints were there.

Let us never be so frantic in our widowhood that we push away the love of those who reach out to us.

The Fifth Station: Simon Helps Jesus Carry the Cross

Mary ...

You wished you could carry that cross for Your Son. You must have sighed in relief to see Simon bearing the weight.

As widows, even after many years, we can feel lonely, overwhelmed, and hopeless, desperately wishing for help.

Holy Mary, pray for your daughters in our hour of need.

Jesus, You are the God-man, yet You let another help when You were unable to keep going. Why, then, should we be too proud to beg? So often a cry brings assistance that does not come to those who hide their weakness.

In the Scriptures, the Holy Spirit promises rewards to those who aid widows. Show us who can help us in our neediness ... and, when there really is no one, let us always fall back on You, the Second Bridegroom of widows. Strengthen our backs even as the cross still weighs us down.

Sixth Station: Veronica Wipes the Face of Jesus

Mary ...

Most likely you knew this valiant disciple, and saw the imprint of your Son's face on that cloth long after His ascension.

Did you wipe the face of St. Joseph, just as we wiped the brow of our beloved husbands in their final moments? Did the image of your husband's face remain with you long after? When words can do little, gestures can do much.

All of us treasure the image of our husbands, if not on a cloth, then in photographs. Holy Mary, pray for us as we remember.

Jesus, we hope our husbands asked forgiveness for their sins before their deaths, even if we did not witness this. We believe that they are either in purgatory or heaven. The fully resurrected body will not be theirs – or ours – until the Last Judgment. Yet, as we struggle along without our husbands, we like to imagine their faces looking down on us with compassion, and often, humor.

Seventh Station: Jesus Falls the Second Time

Mary... refuge of sinners...

More than any other witness, you understood how the cross of Jesus was part of the Father's plan of salvation.

As your Son fell again, did you think of us sinners, through the centuries, coming to repentance? In your great distress, did your heart rejoice to see us repenting as we prayed these very stations?

During our long widowhood we have ample time to remember how often we fell from grace, when our own faults and sins hurt our spouses.

Mother Mary, pray for us your daughters, as we look to God for mercy.

Jesus, give us courage to confess the major sins of our married lives in the sacrament of reconciliation. You want us to have peace. Help us to believe that, in eternity, our husbands have repented of their sins against us. They do not judge us harshly now, for the are participating in the compassionate love of Your Sacred Heart for themselves and for us.

Eighth Station: The Women Console Jesus

Mary ...

Were the women who braved the jeering crowd to console Jesus on the way of the cross the same women who surrounded you when Joseph died? Surely, they would not have left the mother of Love alone at her hour of need!

When we first became widows, more seasoned widows came forward to comfort and inspire us with their survival skills and their trust in you and in Jesus.

Holy Mary, pray for us with the compassion of your mother's heart.

Jesus, deep is the consolation you wish to pour into our frazzled and forlorn widowed hearts. You would have us know that we are never, never, never, alone. But we need much grace to stretch ourselves beyond our senses to know You now in an even more intimate spiritual way than before. Only You can settle us down in the peace that comes with Your presence.

Ninth Station: Jesus Falls Again

Mary ...

Despite your unique and exalted privilege as Mother of God, you must have felt your status in the world fall when you were no longer "Joseph's wife" but only a poor widow.

In our times, most of us grieve our new state each time we fill out a form and are forced to check the "widow" box instead of the "married" box. Sometimes our social life falls because we are not part of a couple. Often, our income falls as well.

Mother Mary, pray for us your daughters as we feel our place in the world diminish.

Jesus, throughout Scripture, Your people were exhorted to honor needy widows. Purify the minds of all widows from negative images of widowhood. Show us if You want to provide us with second husbands. In Your new covenant, we are offered a new consecrated state, living to serve Your church. If our new vocation is to have You as our Second Bridegroom, show us how.

Tenth Station: Jesus is Stripped

Mary ...

Did you keep any of your Son's things after His death? Perhaps you even kept some of Joseph's belongings. We cannot know for certain. What we do know is that Jesus was parted from his clothes by force, an act of violence.

After the death of our husbands, it was a painful process to go through their possessions. As we stripped away those clothes, we felt the memories connected to those clothes slip away as well.

In another sense we feel stripped of everything our husband's presence meant to us, especially on anniversaries, birthdays, family holidays, and religious holy days. Holy Mary, pray for your daughters as we struggle to place all our losses into the hands of God.

Jesus: You wept at the death of Lazarus – and though it is not recorded, no doubt You cried when Joseph died, too. Even so, You also told us not to grieve as unbelievers do. Grief takes many forms; some of these forms are surprising, such as mourning over an article of our husband's clothing. We beg You to turn each experience of loss into gratitude for the good times.

We hope for that day when our resurrected bodies will be clothed in unimaginable splendor, and we will be reunited with our loved ones. In the meantime, give us grace to be glad to be stripped of what we no longer need, and to help those who have less, especially the starving and homeless.

Eleventh Station: Jesus is Nailed to the Cross

Mary ...

You had to watch your Son endure one of the worst deaths ever devised. You saw the nails, blood, wounds, and his horrible, agonizing pain. At the crucifixion, you reflected the pain and strain your Son was experiencing. You became a mirror of His crucifixion.

Many widows recall having witnessed the awful, gut-wrenching miseries of a husband's suffering. Like you, Mary, we became mirrors of that suffering. Our faces, previously more often expressive of light hearted joy, now manifest the heavy sadness of death.

Jesus, through our baptism each of us is incorporated into the Paschal mystery. This means that, like You, we will all experience the passion, death and resurrection. Seen in this light, the loss of our husbands unites us to You in a profound way. Your mother shows us how to endure our cross and how to unite it to Yours. Help us to use our suffering and grief as a conduit of redemptive love that can lead others to You. Mary, our Mother, pray for us now and at the hour of death.

Twelfth Station: Jesus Dies on the Cross

Mary ...

How often the ways of God must have surprised you, from the Annunciation and through all the mysteries of your life. Perhaps as Jesus

166

was being crucified, you waited expectantly for another miracle, hoping that somehow the resurrection would occur right then.

But that did not happen. Instead, Jesus gave you another unexpected gift: the gift of spiritual motherhood. You were to become mother of His Church, symbolized in the person of John, the beloved apostle.

Jesus: even in the last moments, we prayed for our husband's healing and health. Even when they died suddenly, without warning, we prayed over their bodies hoping that they, like Lazarus, could be raised from the dead. We wanted them to remain with us here on earth.

As we pray for the souls of our husbands, we are reminded that there is still work that You have for us to do. As we mourn, let our tears never blind us to the need for love in the people around us.

Thirteenth Station: Jesus is Taken from the Cross

Mary ...

Great artists and sculptors have depicted the tender moment when you held the body of Jesus for the last time. Did you also remember holding the body of St. Joseph for the last time? How often we wish that we could see our husbands again in the flesh, and embrace them in love.

Pray for us, O Holy Mary, that we might offer these longings back to God. Turn our grief into powerful seeds of prayer.

Jesus, You want us to grieve but not to beg for what is not Your will. Instead of physical contact with our husbands' bodies, You want to stretch us to make contact with them through prayer. Please wean us from wanting what is gone and help us to want what we can have in a spiritual way now and in eternity. Some widows experience the souls of their spouses with them always, and others rarely, if at all. Help us to trust in the signs of eternal life You choose for each of us as individuals. Many of us have found healing graces through groups, each of us as individuals. Many of us have found healing graces through groups on bereavement and grief. If we could benefit from such ministries, help us to overcome our desire to hide our pain. Let us not reject what would bring hope.

Fourteenth Station: Jesus Is Buried

Mary …

Some who write about you believe that Jesus first appeared to you, his mother, privately. We do not know how that was, but we do know that you understand how we feel at the burial of those we love. Even with the numbness that often comes with a death, the farewell at the gravesite is always poignant.

Jesus, You want to increase our faith in life eternal. In the meantime, You teach us to believe in Your mystical body, experienced in its highest form on earth at Holy Mass and in the reception of Holy Communion. Help us to believe that our communion with You at the sacred rites is also a communion with the one to whom we were joined in the sacrament of marriage. You have made saints of some widows, known to us, or hidden from the public eye. What more can we pray for than that, like them, our hearts be free from doubt, bitterness, anxiety, and despair and be filled, instead, with the joys You send us (even as we suffer) and with love, love, and LOVE.

Pop Psychology
and Catholic Spirituality

Unpublished Article

First, some rough definitions of terms:

Psychology, without the "pop" adjective, is the study of the human psyche. Approaches to professional psychology include statistical experimental psychology, Freudian psychoanalysis, Jungian analysis, Gestalt, and many others.

The term "pop psychology" is usually a negative description of a whole range of self-help and group methods for dealing with emotional problems that have developed in the 2nd half of the 20th century and continue into the present time. Groups based on these theories are often led by non-professionals; including Christian counselors who are not professional psychologists.

The term "Catholic spirituality" includes the age-old teachings of our spiritual masters such as those of St. Benedict, St. Francis, St. Ignatius of Loyola, St. Teresa of Avila, St. John of the Cross, St. Francis de Sales, and many others.

Two Current Attitudes about Pop Psychology

The Case Against the Use of Pop Psychology for Christian Counselors

Pop psychology is a ridiculous substitute for spirituality and is especially hateful because many Sisters who got into it in the 1960's and '70's, left their religious communities. Especially annoying is the Pelagian excess in some pop psychological systems which seem to promise that "if you just figure out your personality type, or join our self-help group, you will live happily ever after in time and in eternity!" As well, there can be a tendency of participants to label others in an uncharitable manner, and to excuse themselves as simply acting out the "type" they have learned fits them. Professional Christian psychologists are often concerned that use of such self-help and group systems keeps people who greatly need professional help from taking advantage of it. The Catholic Psychotherapy Association, for example, offers professional care that can be trusted.

The Case for Use of Pop Psychology with Christian Counselors

Pop psychology is terrific. Without paying often expensive fees of psychologists for long treatments, I can use psychological concepts to analyze my friends, my enemies, and myself. Pop psychologies explain everything that is wrong with me and give me handy tools for improvement.

A Third Approach

Instead of either of these alternative attitudes toward pop psychology, I want to show how we can use selected truths in tandem with professional counseling and spiritual direction in a good way to help us understand others and ourselves. One can avoid labelling and excusing oneself, in synthesis with still deeper classical spirituality.

Skeptical?

Maybe you are thinking that since classical spirituality is so deep and beautiful, why get into pop psychology at all? But, then, how is that some Catholics who go to Daily Mass and pray an hour a day minimum, still have glaring faults which victimize those they love, such as health destroying addictions, toxic anger, obsessive anxiety, and non-clinical depression?

By analogy, just because a healing miracle is more beautiful, we don't avoid getting a flu shot. Grace perfects nature, it doesn't usually substitute for it.

And there really are good Catholic psychologists, trained pastoral counselors and spiritual directors who use some of the concepts of pop psychology in tandem with classical spirituality.

EXAMPLES OF CONCEPTS IN POP PSYCHOLOGY IN RELATION TO CLASSICAL SPIRITUALITY

Here are some examples of how this can work.

Myers-Briggs Personality Typology

It was in the '70's that the Myers-Briggs Personality typology became well-known. It is based on Jungian personality concepts. The popular book I found most helpful was called *Please Understand Me* by David Keirsey and Marilyn Bates. Basically, people can be divided between these contrasting approaches to life:

According to this topology, there are four pairs of psychological traits. They are:

(E) EXTROVERT or (I) INTROVERT
(N) INTUITIVE or (S) SENSATE
(T) THINKING or (F) FEELING
(J) JUDGING or (P) PERCEIVING

A necessary distinction: most people are primarily one or the other of these polarities, but not exclusively

- FIRST PAIR: Some people gain energy from being with people (extrovert); others gain energy being alone (introvert).
- SECOND PAIR: Some persons perceive the world in a more abstract manner (intuitive); others perceive the world in a more concrete sensory manner).
- THIRD PAIR: Some persons prefer to make their decisions based in their thought about an issue (thinking), others prefer to decide based on emotions (feeling).
- FOURTH PAIR: Some persons prefer to act on what they perceive as orderly, (judging); others prefer flexibility, playing it by ear (perception).

You can google Myers-Briggs and read a lot more about these types.

To illustrate how understanding such a typology can be synthesized with classical spirituality I will focus on the last contrast as I understand it.

The judging person wants to figure things out and then judge correctly the best way to organize the day, the week, and his/her entire life if possible. By contrast the perceiving person likes to let reality unfold and respond as it goes along. In simpler parlance, the "J" personality will tend to be highly efficient but, in the negative, tends to micro-managing others. The "P" personality will tend to be easy-going but, in the negative, is often late and hard to pin down to a straight answer.

When I became familiar with this personality contrast, I had to realize that I was the most "J" in my family, and that one of the others, my husband, tested out extremely "P." How could I be willing to put up with his laid-back ways I had to deal with every day?

With a lot of struggle over a long time I came to accept his laid-back ways, learned to work around those ways. I came to realize that even

I found my laid-back family and friends more pleasurable to be with than dealing with some other people as highly organized as myself! As I liked to quip after my husband's departure for eternal life, "Becoming a widow often means realizing that the absence of annoyance is not joy!"

So, how does this relate to classical spirituality? There is no way that the Christian life is based on the smooth sailing of perfectly organized life on earth! Acceptance of unavoidable sufferings, large and small, applies not only to physical crosses, but also to personality conflicts. Can you imagine opening a book of St. Teresa of Avila and finding a teaching that spiritual peace comes with criticizing, berating, and rejecting everyone who is not just like yourself? No. Peace comes, in such cases, from such prayers as offering the unavoidable sufferings that come with such conflicts for the conversion of the world.

Now, a second example of pop psychology working with Catholic spirituality.

Recovery, International: for Anger, Anxiety and Depression

Not 12 Step, also called Recovery, this system of group meetings was started in the 1950s by Dr. Abraham Low, a psychiatrist in Chicago. Low was Jewish but not religious. He discovered that patients who made progress when in the Institution, once released, couldn't cope with daily life. He gradually developed a system of weekly group meetings that has since become world-wide with non-professional leaders of many nationalities.

In 1994 I started going to one of the groups of Recovery, International at Franciscan University of Steubenville, where I was teaching. The reason was anger. There was hardly a time after I became a Catholic in 1959 that anger wasn't part of my monthly confession of sins.

You can read about the philosophy of Abraham Low regarding dealing with negative emotions on the Recovery, International website. For our purposes here, I want to highlight a subtle concept of Abraham Low that any angry person can benefit from pondering.

According to Dr. Low, we are angry because we feel actually harmed or potentially harmed by another person or situation, ranging all the way from being rejected to being treated unjustly, or frustrated in daily life goals, to dealing with a bad driver who could cause you to die in an accident.

Now, this anger includes a feeling of weakness when we don't have the power to change that situation. However, when we act out of anger, we feel strong, even when we have not actually won any victory over the offending party. Low calls this mechanism getting a merely "symbolic victory."

Take a few examples; not necessarily mine:

My candidate for President didn't win the election. I am angry because I fear horrible consequences from the victory of the opponent. I feel weak. I have no power to reverse that election. But, now, I sit with my political allies and we ridicule the victor. Nothing changes, but we have a temporary feeling of strength. We "be-little" the enemy. We have a symbolic victory.

A group of suburban housewives meets for coffee together every morning after their husbands leave for their commute to work. Many of these women feel frustrated and angry because their husbands won't do everything they want in the house, such as fixing broken things, or disciplining the children. They feel powerless to get their husbands to do what they want. But, at the coffee-klatch, each wife, when telling the others how their husbands ignored their demands, feels strong. Instead of being the weak wife, she is now the judge. Nothing changes. She gets no real victory, but she gets a symbolic victory.

A man is driving on the freeway. He sees a crazy speeding car zig-zagging from lane to lane 20 mph above the speed limit. He gets agry. He is in the weak position because there is nothing he can do to stop the other driver. He is weak. But, if the driver comes near him and he screams out a curse or gives the other driver "the finger," he feels strong. Not a real victory, but a symbolic victory since, in his imagination, he has punished the other driver with his curse. Think of the common angry words: "go to hell!"

So, what is Low's remedy? In the weekly group, the members report daily occurrences where anger, anxiety, or depression played a role. Then they relate the incident to one of the common-sense tools they have been taught to use. There are some 50 or more of such sayings but here are a few:

- "Expect frustrations every 5 minutes, you won't be disappointed."

- "If you can't change a situation, you can change your attitude toward it."
- "Inner success in controlling your emotions is more important than outer success."
- "It's not a 911."

After about 10 years of being in such weekly groups, led by non-professional group leaders, I went from 5 fits of anger a day to, maybe, 2 a week. I wrote a book called *Taming the Lion Within: 5 Steps from Anger to Peace* (St. Louis, Missouri: En Route Books and Media, 2017) relating the insights of Recovery, International to Catholic spirituality.

Here is one of the key formulations I made use of in my book. Even if I go to daily Mass and pray an hour a day, if I have the attitude I will now describe, I will be angry, anxious or depressed all day long. What is this attitude? If I think that I am the star of the drama of life and everyone else is a secondary character or a cameo, since they will refuse these roles, I will be angry at them for not saying and doing what I want, or anxious that they won't, or depressed because they didn't. Instead, I have to come to see God as the star of reality, and myself as the secondary character, enhancing His role in building the kingdom of God.

And, what is classical spirituality about if not how to be a child of God instead of a proud pseudo-king or queen in the kingdom of this world?

12 Steps Anonymous for Addictions

How many of you readers gag, as I do, when someone says, "I am not religious, but I am spiritual"?

Some who so describe themselves are coming out of "12 Step spirituality". This is because many are former members of Christian churches, but they have come to some sense of a "Higher Power". I don't think that most of them left a church because of 12 Step. Rather, they left long ago and then discovered 12 Step.

However, for some, 12 Step is a bridge back to membership in Christian churches, and some of the original non-psychologist leaders were and remained strong Catholics.

Started so many years ago to help alcoholics, this movement has spread to include other addictions such as narcotics, nicotine, co-dependency, over-eating, and more recent ones such as Shopaholics Anonymous, Emotions Anonymous, and Hoarders anonymous.

Attending meetings of Al-Anon for relatives of Alcoholics, I became familiar with the popular psychological concepts underlying this world-wide movement.

When the addict admits that his or her life is out of control and surrenders to the Higher Power, the members of the group, usually very gradually, come to let go of the addiction and replace it with a sensible life. A combination of divine grace and pop psychology!

Now, in all classical Catholic spirituality, a central role is played by detachment. There is no way to become holy if we have inordinate attachment to any worldly good. A holy person can certainly have an alcoholic beverage, a delicious meal, close friends, and needed possessions. But clinging to anything as more important than obeying the will of God in any circumstance where there is a conflict is an obstacle to holiness.

So why not just cling to God in Church and beg to be freed of any addictions we might have? Certainly, that is possible. Saints such as the Irish recovered alcoholic, Matt Talbot, were freed from addiction before AA was around.

However, what church-going members of 12 Step groups report is that the intensity of the fellowship at the weekly meetings of people with the same addiction can be the key to eventual detachment. Also, the members who do have a strong Catholic spirituality can witness, albeit discreetly, and become sponsors to help others.

Conclusion

But, but, but...you might be thinking, "It's nice you had such happy, helpful experiences with popular psychology, but I am uncomfortable with all those personality labels and those groups giving a stage to egomaniacs!"

I find that for those who dislike group meetings face to face, going to an online or phone group for the same issues can be easier. Google the name of your addiction to find the groups and the modes of participation.

On the other hand, some of the same benefits of greater insight into our problems and other great spiritual benefits can come from finding a good spiritual guide who is conversant with psychology and spirituality, though not a paid specialist – professional in either subject.

Trained pastoral counselors and spiritual directors, whether priests, brothers, sisters, or lay people, can help one get to the root of what blocks our emotional and religious growth. But, if such cannot be found in the area where you live, a friend who is further along the road to holiness can be extremely helpful if you are humble enough to get out of denial and be radically open about your problems.

Here are two short examples from my own experience about this.

Some years back, an expert in lay Ignatian retreats took me through a whole year of meditations. Even more critical was how in his own prayer for me he was able to pinpoint specific flaws of character that were blocking my spiritual growth. Guess what? One of these was the tendency to substitute psychological analysis of others for more simply praying to be an instrument of love for them: praying ardently to God for graces to come upon them.

Recently, I asked for spiritual direction from a friend who is not a practicing professional of psychology. Al Hughes, M.S., M.P.M. is a Benedictine-trained lay pastoral counselor, spiritual director, catechist, retreat master and author.

The methods he used with moderate success and the progress we made is related in our book called *Escaping Anxiety along the Road to Spiritual Joy,* by Albert E. Hughes and Ronda Chervin (St. Louis, Missouri, En Route Books and Media, 2018). The psychological part was getting to what Hughes calls "the bitter root judgment" underlying my anxiety. In my case, anxiety was rooted in a childhood feeling of being rejected by my father. Then, Hughes led me to overcome anxiety through surrender to the permissive will of God found in the realities of the present time in my life.

My prayer as I conclude the writing of this article is this: Father God, we thank you for all the wisdom through the ages from Christian spiritual masters. We thank you for the truths to be found in other writings and groups, as well. Help us to avoid pitfalls of popular psychology taken as a substitute for Your truth, but may we not, on the other hand, ignore any insights that could help us to become more healed sisters and brothers in Your kingdom.

Books by Ronda Chervin
Arranged by Date of Publication

Church of Love (Liguori, Missouri: Liguori Publications), 1972. (Part of this became a booklet published by St. Paul Books and Media called *Signs of Love: How Jesus Loves us through the Sacraments*, 1989.)

The Art of Choosing: Guidelines for Making Life Decisions (Liguori, Missouri: Liguori Publications), 1974.

Prayer and Your Everyday Life Series, including 3 booklets: *Prayer and Your Everyday Life, The Spirit and your Everyday Life* and *Love and your Everyday Life* (Liguori: Missouri: Liguori Publications), 1975.

Why I am a Charismatic: A Catholic Explains (Liguori, Missouri: Liguori Publications), 1978.

The Way, the Truth and the Life: Meeting Christ in Prayer (Pecos, New Mexico: Dove Publications), 1978.

The Woman's Tale: A Journal of Inner Exploration (with co-author Mary Neill) (New York: Seabury), 1981.

Bringing the Mother with You: Sources of Healing in Marian Meditation (with co-author Mary Neill) (New York: Seabury Press), 1982.

How Shall We Find the Father: Meditations for Mixed Voices (with co-authors Mary Neill and Don Briel) (New York: The Seabury Press), 1983.

Half-Way to Eternity: Prayer-Poems (Sedona, Arizona: Chiaro-Oscuro Press), 1983.

Victory Over Death: Foretastes of Eternity in Prayer (Petersham, Massachusetts: St. Bede's Publications), 1985.

The Holy Dybbuk: Letters of Charles Rich, Contemplative (Petersham, Massachusetts: St. Bede's Publications), 1988.

Great Saints, Great Friends (with co-author Mary Neill, OP) (Staten Island, N.Y.: Alba House), 1989.

Hungry for Heaven: The Story of Charles Rich, Contemplative (Petersham, Massachusetts, St. Bede's Publications), 1993.

Feminine, Free and Faithful (San Francisco: Ignatius Press), 1987. (Reprinted by Franciscan University Press, Steubenville, Ohio), 1995. (Published in Spanish under the title *Femeninas, Libres y Fieles* by Editorial Diana in 1991.)

The Ingrafting: The Conversion Stories of Ten Hebrew Catholics (Petersham, Massachusetts: St. Bede's Publications), 1987.

Living in Love: Christian Ethics for Everyday Life (Boston: St. Paul's Books and Media), 1988. (This book is reprinted as part of a 4-volume compendium entitled *The Way of Love,* published in 2013.)

Love of Wisdom: An Introduction to Christian Philosophy (with co-author Msgr. Eugene Kevane) (San Francisco: Ignatius Press), 1988.

Woman to Woman (with co-author Terri Vorndran Nichols) (San Francisco: Ignatius Press), 1988.

Prayers of the Women Mystics (Ann Arbor, Michigan: Servant), 1992. (Published in Italian under the title *Le Preghiere delle Grandi Mistiche* in 1992.)

Spiritual Friendship: Darkness and Light (Boston: St. Paul's Books and Media), 1992.

Tell My Why: Answering Tough Questions about the Faith (with co-author Msgr. Joseph Pollard) (Huntington, Indiana: Our Sunday Visitor), 1994.

En Route to Eternity: The Story of My Life (New York: Miriam Press), 1994.

A Mother's Treasury of Prayers (Ann Arbor, Michigan: Servant), 1994.

Treasury of Women Saints (Ann Arbor, Michigan: Servant Publications), 1991. (Reprinted and updated by Franciscan Media, 2015.) (Translated into Italian under the title *Donne Sante,* published by Libreria Editrice Vaticana in 1995.)

Quotable Saints (Ann Arbor, Michigan: Servant), 1992. (Reprinted by CMJ Marian Publishers.)

The Book of Catholic Customs and Traditions, (with co-author Carla

Conley) (Ann Arbor, Michigan: Servant Publications), 1994.

The Kiss from the Cross: A Saint for Every Kind of Suffering (Ann Arbor, Michigan: Servant Publications), 1994. (Published in Korean in 2000.) (Reprinted in 2015 under the title *Avoiding Bitterness in Suffering: How Our Heroes in Faith Found Peace amid Sorrow* by Sophia Institute Press (Manchester, New Hampshire), 2015.

Freed to Love: Healing for Catholic Women (Sedona, Arizona: ChiaroOscuro Press), 1994.

Bread from Heaven: Stories of Jews who found the Messiah (New Hope, Kentucky, Remnant of Israel), 1994.

Letters for Eternity: Collected from the Correspondence of Charles Rich with Ronda Chervin (Petersham, Massachusetts: St. Bede's Publications), 1994.

Voyage to Insight (with co-author Lois August Janis) (Sedona, Arizona: Chiaro-Oscuro Press), 1994. (Reprinted by En Route Books, 2014.)

Becoming a Handmaid of the Lord: From the Journals of Ronda De Sola Chervin 1977-1996 (Oak Lawn, Illinois: CMJ Associates), 1997.

Holding Hands with God: Catholic Women Share Their Stories of Courage and Hope (Huntington, Indiana: Our Sunday Visitor), 1997.

A Widow's Walk: Encouragement, Comfort, and Wisdom from the Widow-Saints (Huntington, Indiana: Our Sunday Visitor), 1998. (This was reprinted in a revised edition with Heidi Hess Saxton, related more to grieving by Simon Peter Press, under the title *Walk with Me, Jesus: A Widow's Journey*, in 2008.)

Healing Meditations from the Gospel of St. John (with co-author Dr. Ross Porter) (Oak Lawn, Illinois: CMJ – Marian Publishers), 2000.

The Fabric of Our Lives (Oak Lawn: CMJ Marian Publishers), 2000.

Seeking Christ in the Crosses and Joys of Aging (Oak Lawn, Illinois: CMJ – Marian Publishers), 2000.

Help in Time of Need: Encouragement, Practical Advice and Prayers (Ann Arbor, Michigan: Servant), 2002.

Taming the Lion Within: 5 Steps from Anger to Peace (Oldsmar, Florida: Simon Peter Press), 2003.

Legacy: How to Share the Memories You Treasure with Family and Friends (Oak Lawn, Illinois: CMJ Marian Publications), 2005.

What the Saints Said About Heaven (with co-authors Richard and Ruth Ballard) (Charlotte, North Carolina: TAN/St. Benedict), 2011.

Last Call: Twelve Men Who Dared Answer, Stories of Late Vocations to the Priesthood (Corpus Christi, Texas: Goodbooksmedia), 2012.

Toward a 21st Century Catholic World-View (Corpus Christi, Texas: Goodbooksmedia), 2014.

Catholic Realism: A Framework for the Refutation of Atheism and the Evangelization of Atheists, (with co-author Sebastian Mahfood) (St. Louis, Missouri: En Route Books and Media), 2015.

Spirituality for All Times: Readings from the Catholic Classics (with co-author Kathleen Brouillette) (St. Louis, Missouri: En Route Books and Media), 2015.

Weeping with Jesus: The Journey from Grief to Hope (St. Louis, Missouri: En Route Books and Media), 2016.

Healing from Rejection with the Help of the Lord: A Survivor's Guide (En Route Books) (St. Louis, Missouri: En Route Books and Media), 2016.

The Way of Love: The Battle for Inner Transformation (including *What is Love: Obstacles to Love, Making Loving Moral Decisions, and 100 Day Spiritual Marathon)* (St. Louis, Missouri: En Route Books and Media), 2017,

Why I am Still a Catholic, a series of booklets edited by Ronda Chervin including one authored by her (Corpus Christi, Texas: Goodbooksmedia.com), 2017.

Escaping Anxiety on the Road to Spiritual Joy (with co-author Al Hughes) (St. Louis, Missouri: En Route Books and Media), 2018.

Simple Holiness (with co-author Al Hughes) (St. Louis, Missouri, En Route Books and Media), 2018.

9 Toes in Eternity (Corpus Christi, Texas: Goodbooksmedia.com), 2018.

Road Map for 80-Year-Olds (with co-author Al Hughes) (St. Louis, Missouri: En Route Books and Media), 2019.

Short-Takes. Transcripts of WCAT Radio Shows edited by Ronda Chervin (St. Louis, Missouri: En Route Books and Media), 2019.

Give Me Your Heart: Preparing for Eternal Life – From the Writings of Charles Rich. Edited by Ronda Chervin (St. Louis, Missouri: En Route Books and Media), 2019.

The Battle for the 20th Century Mind (St. Louis, Missouri: En Route Books and Media), 2001.

Always a New Beginning: A Conversation between Broken Spiritual Warriors (St. Louis, Missouri: En Route Books and Media), 2020.

Self-Published:

Becoming a Woman of God: Your 15 -Week Guided Journal, with co-author Eileen Spotts, 1995.

Ties that Bind: The Story of a Marriage (a novel), 1995.

The Summer Knight's Tale (with co-author Gene Grandy) (a novel), 2001.

The Last Fling (a novel), 2002.

Called by Name: Following a Personal Spirituality, 2006.

God Alone! Solo Dios Basta – Thoughts Received by Ronda Chervin, 2008.

6 Toes in Eternity – Journals of Ronda Chervin, 2018

www.ingramcontent.com/pod-product-compliance
Lightning Source LLC
Chambersburg PA
CBHW031843090426
42741CB00005B/333